Maternal Activism

SUNY series, Praxis: Theory in Action

Nancy A. Naples, editor

Maternal Activism

Mothers Confronting Injustice

DANIELLE POE

Published by State University of New York Press, Albany

For information, contact State University of New York Press, Albany, NY
www.sunypress.edu

Production, Eileen Nizer
Marketing, Michael Campochiaro

Library of Congress Cataloging-in-Publication Data

Poe, Danielle.
    Maternal activism : mothers confronting injustice / Danielle Poe.
        pages cm. — (SUNY series, praxis: theory in action)
    Includes bibliographical references and index.
    ISBN 978-1-4384-5571-6 (hardcover : alk. paper)
    ISBN 978-1-4384-5572-3 (ebook)
    1. Mothers—Political activity.   2. Women—Political activity.
3. Motherhood—Political aspects.   4. Political participation—Moral and
ethical aspects.   I. Title.

    HQ759.P585 2015
    306.874'3—dc23   2014017093

10 9 8 7 6 5 4 3 2 1

Dedicated to Claire Poe:
Thank you, Mom, for your support of my work
And for always inspiring me!

Contents

Acknowledgments

Earlier versions of the following chapters appeared originally in the following publications. A version of Chapter 2 first appeared in 2010 as, "Mothers' Civil Disobedience" in the *Journal of Peace and Justice Studies*, 19(2), 27–45. Chapter 3 has been adapted and developed from "Woman, Mother, and Nonviolent Activism" in *Positive Peace: Reflections on Peace Education, Nonviolence, and Social Change*, edited by Andrew Fitz-Gibbon, New York, New York: Rodopi Press, 119–132. The section entitled "Truth," in Chapter 4 is revised from "Reality America," in *The Mississippi Review*, Winter 2005. Chapter 5 was modified from "Mothering Against the Norms: Diane Wilson and Environmental Activism" in *Incarcerated Mothers: Oppression and Resistance*, edited by Rebecca Bromwich and Gordana Eljdupovic, Toronto, Ontario: Demeter Press (2013). I gratefully acknowledge each of these presses for allowing me to reprint the modified versions of my work here.

I would like to thank the University of Dayton, Department of Philosophy and the College of Arts and Sciences for supporting the work I have done on this book. In particular, Dean Paul Benson who encouraged me to apply for a sabbatical in order to complete this work, and Professor John Inglis, Department of Philosophy, who was also instrumental in helping me to apply for a sabbatical to complete this work.

Within the Department of Philosophy, I would like to thank Professor Patricia Johnson, who was instrumental in creating a department that values diverse philosophical perspectives and strong representation of women philosophers. She, along with Professor Marilyn Fischer, read drafts of my work over the years and they have been mentors in the philosophy profession and within the University of Dayton.

My thanks also go out to Diane Dunham and Karen Slattery; their attention to detail and quick turnaround while editing helped make this book possible.

Biography as Philosophy

The Power of Personal Example
for Transformative Theory

As I have written this book, my kids have always been present in some way. Sometimes, they are literally present because they are beside me playing, asking questions, wanting my attention. Other times, they are present in the background of my consciousness because I'm thinking about the world they live in and the kind of world I want them to live in. Our life together is probably familiar to many U.S. middle-class women: I work full-time, the kids go to school full time, and our evenings and weekends are filled with a range of activities with which we are each involved. We stay busy with our individual activities, but we also come together for dinner most nights, we go on family outings, and we enjoy our time together. As much time as I do spend with my kids, I constantly feel guilty for not doing enough with them since I also spend significant time preparing for classes, grading, researching, and writing while I'm with them. Along with many other women, I feel the pressure of trying and failing to balance mothering and a career.

Although I feel as though I could be a better mother and a better academic, I also have to concede that I lead a privileged life as a woman and mother. Mothers around the world would love to have the luxury of providing for their children's physical and mental well-being. In the Ivory Coast and Ghana, children are used as slave labor to harvest cocoa beans for chocolate (Bitter Truth; "FLA Highlights"; Hawksley; The Food Empowerment Project). In Uganda, children are kidnapped for military service where they are tortured and forced to commit atrocities ("Lords of Woe"; History; Bangura; Doom; Lane; Vindevogel). In Peru, children's health has been devastated by the mining of heavy metals, which has produced high levels of sulfur dioxide and lead (Fraser).

Mothers in these countries—and mothers who face poverty, violence, and racism in the United States—face daily uncertainties about whether their children will be safe, fed, and healthy.

My heart aches for these children and these mothers, especially when I stop to consider the daily life of my children and me contributes to their suffering. As part of the U.S. middle-class, to say nothing of the wealthy, we go through our daily routines without thinking about the supply chain that produces our goods. We fail to think of the children who produced the soccer balls and the chocolate we enjoy. Far too many of us have no idea that the people who mine the materials used to make our computers, cell phones, and mp3 players are exploited and oppressed. Yet, simply feeling sad for others' plight and guilty for my own role does nothing to stop the exploitation and the violence those mothers and children face every day, so I find myself constantly searching for ways to critique this system of injustice, to raise questions about the lives of people impacted by my acts, and to create a just, peaceful world. Moreover, I want to use my experience as a mother to cultivate the connection between myself and other mothers and their children. In order to foster this connection, I began by looking for other U.S. mothers who recognized systemic injustice, critiqued the injustice, and worked to make the world more just.

Molly Rush, Michele Naar-Obed, Cindy Sheehan, and Diane Wilson

In my search for what it means to be a mother who cares about the suffering of others and acts to alleviate that suffering, I discovered four mothers whose experiences led them to care about the plight of people around them, both those in their own communities and those across the world. Even more importantly, that care led them to act to change the injustice they discovered. By focusing on individual mothers and the implications of their stories, I found that the critiques of essentialism receded since they each have particular ways of assessing and responding to the injustice that they discover. Their responses share features with other women and mothers and can provide inspiration and insight without imposing a universal standard of what it means to be a mother.

The contributions of particular mothers is important because it addresses a tension that runs through scholarship about organizations built on the idea of a natural connection between mothering and peace.

The tension is between the idea that mothers have a special insight into the destruction that war causes and that such an insight relies on oppressive stereotypes about women and mothers. Michelle Moravec articulates this tension in her article "Another Mother for Peace: Reconsidering Maternalist Peace Rhetoric from a Historical Perspective, 1967–2007" (2010). Moravec argues that "Ultimately, while motherhood provides an emotionally resonate call for motivating peace activists, it undercuts the political efficacy of women working to end war" (10). Her argument is that groups such as Another Mother for Peace and CODEPINK (we can also add GSFSO) use essentialist descriptions of mothers to try to garner support for the peace movement. She does grant that the examples she uses in this article also undermine essentialist categories, but she maintains that overall these groups and individuals are reduced to making essentialist claims. She further argues that this strategy backfires because their message is ultimately ignored by the media or reduced to pity for an individual's suffering, both of which fail to incite critical conversations about militarism and structural injustice. Moravec suggests that to raise these conversations women must be part of coalitions larger than those defined by maternalism (22–29).

The problem Moravec identifies of using essentialist claims about mothering to critique injustice is one that is well documented by Harriet Hyman Alonso in *Peace as a Women's Issue: A History of the U.S. Movement for World Peace and Women's Rights* (1993). She traces, throughout the history of women's peace groups, the pervasiveness of motherhood as a theme of the movement (11–12, 165, 263). As with Moravec's analysis, Alonso recognizes the emotional power of making a link between the ideals of motherhood and pacifism, but she repeatedly critiques the essentialism inherent in the rhetoric (14, 263). The essentialism noted by both Moravec and Alonso are problematic for groups who are organized around the common theme of motherhood and nonviolence. Nevertheless, the number of organizations and activists founded by women and informed by mothering indicate that, while women should not be reduced to essentialist stereotypes, many women can find inspiration from mothering to become activists. I will discuss four such women to emphasize the ways in which mothering inspires their actions without reducing them to one-dimensional stereotypes.

First, I discovered Molly Rush, mother of six, who became a convicted felon when she hammered the nosecone of a nuclear warhead in order to draw attention to the danger of nuclear weapons. Her story, which I will discuss in Chapter 2, led me to consider the ethical ambiguity inherent in mothering. On the one hand, Sara Ruddick's research focuses on the virtues of maternal work and how that work can contribute to living peacefully. On the other hand, mothers who challenge the status quo threaten what society deems acceptable for mothering practices. In order to consider the difficulties of practicing the virtues of mothering in a militaristic society and how these difficulties can be addressed, I focus on the example of Rush and the ethical philosophy of Simone de Beauvoir.

Rush became active in civil rights in 1963 as part of the Catholic Interracial Council in Pittsburgh, Pennsylvania. As part of her commitment to civil rights, she began marching against the Vietnam War the following year (Faulk). By 1980 her awareness of injustice, her dedication to calling attention to that injustice, and her religious commitment to non-violence led Rush to become part of a nonviolent act of civil disobedience in King of Prussia, Pennsylvania, at the General Electric plant where nosecones for nuclear weapons were being produced. Rush and seven others (including two priests and a religious sister) who were part of Plowshares—a Catholic community devoted to nonviolent civil disobedience—walked into the facility, spilled their own blood on the nosecone, and used hammers to destroy it. Another Plowshares member, Art Laffin, describes the dual significance of the blood and hammers:

> Hammers are used to begin the literal dismantling of weapons that rounds of 'peace' talks have failed to do. They are also used to symbolize the 'building again' process, e.g., a hammer can be used to build homes and hospitals. Blood clearly points to the blood that is spilled so carelessly in war. It is also an essential component of life, which points to our need for one another and our unity as one people. (Brown and Muller)

Laffin's description reveals the power of Rush's act as an inspiration for other mothers who want to create a better world. Both the hammers and the blood symbolize critique and renewal. The hammer destroys that which is meant to destroy in order to clear a space for building things that will nourish life. Blood is used to critique the blood that the weapon will spill, but also reminds us of the force of life in every person whether we are in the United States or the then-USSR (the primary intended target of nuclear weapons in 1980).

The use of hammers and blood to emphasize the misplaced values of militarism is a technique used by many feminists. In *Does Khaki*

Become You?: The Militarization of Women's Lives, Cynthia Enloe describes this approach to critiquing militarization as an economic-technological critique (1983). The economic-technological critique can be effective in drawing attention to the ways in which funding militarism impacts other areas of social life so that people will withdraw support for military funding (Enloe 207). A current example of this approach is evident on the website *Cost of War-Trade-Offs*. On this website, viewers can search for the amount of spending on the Afghanistan war for the current fiscal year and compare that spending to what that money could have bought instead. According to this website, taxpayers in the city of Dayton, Ohio (a mid-size American city) will spend $14.12 million dollars in fiscal year 2014 on the Iraq and Afghanistan war, money that could have provided 208 elementary school teachers for one year, medical care for 1,752 military veterans for one year, or a year of health care for 7,549 children from low-income families (National Priorities Project). Although Enloe believes this approach frequently does succeed in convincing people that military expenditures are problematic, it fails to produce a critique of the militarization of society and therefore will not ultimately change the emphasis on war and violence in society (208).

Rush's civil disobedience clearly broadens the category of economic-technological critique since her stated purpose is to wake people up to the reality of the dangers of nuclear weapons, as well as to draw people's attention to the ways in which the production of nuclear weapons detracts from spending and programs that nurture life. Rush was successful in raising people's awareness, bringing about conversations on nuclear weapons, and demonstrating that militarism exists because we let it exist. Yet, Rush did have to serve time, leaving her children without her. Her sacrifice of time with her children and their emotional struggles during her imprisonment highlight the tension that mother-activists face: how can we negotiate the tension between taking care of our particular children and trying to act on behalf of other people suffering, many of whom suffer as a direct result of our failure to act?

After presenting a paper on Rush, an audience member told me about Michele Naar-Obed, who has much in common with Rush, but is able to resolve some of the tension of leaving her child. Naar-Obed, like Rush, hammered the nosecone of a nuclear warhead and is a convicted felon for that act. Both women had to leave their children while they served their sentences, but Rush did so without the support of her husband and community, while Naar-Obed had a robust system of support for herself and her daughter. In Chapter 3, I will focus on Naar-Obed's story of activism and use the theory of Luce Irigaray to explicate the importance of systems of support for activist mothers.

Naar-Obed began her life as an activist during the build-up to the first Iraq War, pouring blood on the building sign of an Air Force recruiting center, and was acquitted after a jury trial for the act. After this first action, Naar-Obed sought out a community that could more fully support her commitment to social justice and non-violent disobedience. She became a member of Jonah House at which time she met and married Greg Boertje-Obed, a fellow activist. Soon after they were married, Naar-Obed and Boertje-Obed had their daughter, Rachel, who would be actively raised not only by the two of them, but also by the Jonah House community (Prisoners of Conscience; Gross; Naar-Obed).

While pregnant with her daughter, Naar-Obed describes seeing pictures of a woman nursing her infant; the woman and child had been burned and bloodied as a result of the nuclear bombs dropped by the U.S. in Japan. She states, "I see that it's me and that baby is mine. For a very brief moment I feel what that mother must have felt. What I feel is just horrendous pain. And I know this cannot be right and it cannot happen again" (Gross 6). Her commitment to making sure this does not happen again leads Naar-Obed, her husband, and the other members of Jonah House to decide she should take part in another act of nonviolent civil disobedience, leaving her two-year-old daughter in the care of her husband and the Jonah House community.

Naar-Obed's story provides an important contrast to Rush's story since Naar-Obed had already been caring for her daughter with the support of a larger community. Nevertheless, her story highlights the tension between social expectations about mothering and personal convictions about the need to confront injustice on behalf of one's own child and every child. Even in a sympathetic article in the *National Catholic Register* about Naar-Obed's peace activism and her relationship with her daughter, the reporter (Judy Gross) asks, "Why are she and other women activists willing to sacrifice their motherhood on the altar of righteousness?" (Gross 5). To answer this question, Gross continues with interviews of Naar-Obed and Liz McAlister (a Jonah House founder, who has also left her children in the care of the community while she served time in prison for her peace activism), and through these interviews it is clear that both consider their actions and time in prison to be integral to their mothering and not a sacrifice of their motherhood. The gap between Naar-Obed's perspective and Gross's initial question demonstrates the need for a community of support for mother-activists so that they can expand what it means to be a mother and to link the well-being of their particular children, to the well-being of all children.

For Naar-Obed, her life as an activist began out of religious commitment and the dissonance of the commitment with the first Iraq War, and her activism expanded when she became a mother. For other mother-activists, activism begins after they are personally impacted by injustice. Cindy Sheehan provides a powerful example of a mother who unexpectedly became a witness to the destruction that war causes. In Chapter 4, I focus on Sheehan's story in order to explicate the ways in which social injustice in the form of U.S. militarism impacts people in ways that they never expected. The aftermath of this impact allows us to examine how activism can begin with a reaction against something that is wrong (the death of a child) and become a proactive activism (a quest to reveal the truth and create a peaceful society). Sheehan's story also provides an opportunity to examine the role of the media in activism since it can bring widespread attention to a cause but it can also marginalize the cause and activists for the cause.

Sheehan was first a mother and only became an activist when her son, Casey, was killed in the second Iraq War. In the aftermath of his death, Sheehan made news across the country, as she demands an account from the president as to the purpose of the Iraq War and the purpose of her son's death. Prior to Casey's death, Sheehan describes herself as a woman whose life centered around her family and her local Catholic Church. While she describes herself and her family as politically active in their opposition to George W. Bush for president, she was not active in political protests or antimilitarism. And, when Casey joined the U.S. Army, Sheehan was deeply troubled by his decision, but she was assured by Casey and the military recruiter that he would not be in harm's way. Until Casey's death, her opposition to the Iraq War and to Bush's presidency remained private political beliefs. But, Casey's death awakened Sheehan's awareness that her private grief is shaped by public policies and systematic misrepresentation of the war and the military. Her private grief, then, becomes public and rallies other peace activists to her cause and catalyzes the media to both honor her and vilify her. Sheehan's transformation into a peace activist raises important questions about the ways in which mothers play a role in shaping their children to become soldiers and support military ideology, the way in which media plays a role in shaping U.S. perceptions of the war and peace activists, and how becoming a mother-activist both ostracizes her from some communities and brings her into solidarity with other communities. From President George W. Bush to members of her extended family, communities with political, economic and emotional stakes in defending the war ostracized Sheehan. CODEPINK, GSFSO, and her surviving children provided sustenance for Sheehan's activism (Knudson; Managhan; Mollin; O'Neill; Rich; Sheehan 2006a; Sheehan 2006b; Sheehan 2005; Wilson; York).

Rush, Naar-Obed, and Sheehan provide inspiration for activism against U.S. militarism and its impact on people around the globe. But as Cynthia Enloe reminds us in *Does Khaki Become You?: The Militarization of Women's Lives*, the influence of militarization traces back to patriarchy (1983, 210), and both patriarchy and militarization have impacts beyond war. Thus, in Chapter 5, I focus on the activism of Diane Wilson, mother of four and tireless activist against war and environmental destruction. Wilson's story demonstrates the ways in which local forms of injustice are linked to global injustice and, while large corporations would have us believe that jobs and progress depend on environmental destruction, that what is good for the environment is also good for people.

As one of the only women shrimpers in Calhoun Bay, Texas, Wilson had been breaking stereotypes for many years. Yet, she was also well-known as someone who valued silence and time alone on her ship; she would never have expected to become an outspoken advocate against corporate pollution, political corruption, and violence. On the day that a fellow shrimper brought her an article about pollution in the bay, Wilson began to ask questions about the levels of pollution that business development would cause. Her questions led her to discover that the environmental damage in her own community was a widespread practice of the corporation in question, and they had left a path of destruction across the United States and around the globe. Nevertheless, politicians and business leaders in her community begged Wilson to stop asking questions and to stop harassing the corporation since they wanted the company to keep operating and to keep building so that they would supposedly provide jobs and development to the community. Wilson continued to challenge the idea that this company provided for the good of the community while it destroyed the livelihood of those who worked on the bay, poisoned many of its workers, and threatened the well-being of the ground and the water for the entire community.

Rather than agree to silence, Wilson continued to ask questions, listen to people harmed, and to connect the injustices perpetrated by the military and corporations, all of which led her to raise other people's awareness of military, environmental, and social injustices through public hunger fasts, disruptions of U.S. Senate hearings and political fund-raisers, and chaining herself to a Union Carbide oxide tower (Wilson 2005; Wilson 2011). Her activism has been instrumental in raising awareness about the connections between local concerns and global concerns, as well as between militarism and environmental destruction.

The focus on each of these individual women, their context, and their actions allow us to better understand how particular individuals can respond to widespread injustice and systemic militarization in society. Each of the mothers in this book does draw on rhetorical strategies that Michelle Moravec labels as essentialist: they appeal to mothers' concern for their children and they use emotivism (10). Nevertheless, they are also undermining essentialism at every turn: they break laws nonviolently; they willingly serve time in jail and prison; and they challenge social standards for acceptability. By studying these individual women and the relationships they form to support their activism, it is clear that maternal activism does not necessarily lead to an essentialist understanding of mothers and women. Rush, Naar-Obed, Sheehan, and Wilson successfully garner media attention, provoke conversations about structural injustice, and incite change as well as challenge preconceived notions of motherhood.

Nonviolent Direct Action

While my first inspiration to write this book came from a desire to help create a just world for my children and other children, I am also deeply committed to nonviolent activism and to teaching people about its effectiveness. A common misunderstanding about nonviolence and peace is a belief that nonviolent actions cannot be effective against conflict and that only violence can be used to stop violence. When I teach students about Jane Addams, Cesar Chavez, Dorothy Day, Martin Luther King, Jr., and Gandhi, I am continually frustrated when they say they admire these peace activists' actions, but that they could never be effective in today's world where people are violent and there is so much cultural conflict. I have had some success using films and articles depicting the violence used against activists and the people they represent, but most students still insist that nonviolence cannot work today, and without violence (war, environmental rape, prisons, social injustice) the world will devolve into chaos and many more instances of violence.

When students worry about increased violence, they tend to think about recent violent events in the United States (9/11 and the bombs at the Boston Marathon, for example). They think that without armed intervention these types of violence will increase and that nonviolence is the equivalent to do nothing. In order to get students and others to consider that nonviolence does work against violence and can create a just society, I use examples from students' daily lives, which can then be expanded so they can understand the motivation and the actions of the activists in this book. For example, Sara Ruddick's analysis of conflict and nonviolence in "Making Connections Between Parenting and Peace" is particularly helpful for introducing the ways in which parents use nonviolence in parenting (2004). In this article, she provides an analysis of conflict and the strategies that parents use to resolve conflicts nonviolently. The examples of nonviolence in this article are familiar to most students and give them a framework from which they can build their capacity to imagine a nonviolent culture and to strengthen their capacity to imagine themselves acting non-violently, both in everyday situations and in the face of cultural violence on a large scale.

Ruddick's insight into the role of nonviolence in the family is an insight that inspires this book as well: we have experiences in our lives that provide the inspiration for creating a just society, the critique of injustice, and the means for moving from injustice toward justice. This book describes the actions of four women (Molly Rush, Michele Naar-Obed, Cindy Sheehan, and Diane Wilson) whose experiences as mothers inspire them to transform society and mothering. While stereotypes of mothering rely on a model of self-sacrifice, nurturing, and caring for their own children within a nuclear family, each of these women expands the institution of mothering beyond these stereotypes by highlighting the connections between all children and all people. Each of these women is nurturing and caring and sacrifices tremendously to create a just peace, but they resist any essential definition of what caring and nurturing entail. While they are willing to take a stand for what is right even when their communities and loved ones urge them to stop, they find and help create supportive communities to share the work of transformation and mothering.

Once students begin to think about the ways in which nonviolence functions in a daily context, the challenge is to get them to think about the role of protests and activism in nonviolence. For the most part students agree with the analysis that Jules Boykoff offers in *Beyond Bullets: The Suppression of Dissent in the United States*:

> Contained, sanctioned actions are not likely to garner mass-media attention, but disruptive, novel events improve the chances of mass-media interest. This relationship with the media creates a dialectic of escalation whereby activists feel perpetually compelled to foment protest activities that are novel and attention-grabbing enough to be newsworthy. Yet, this creates a dilemma in that such actions can be easily dismissible as gimmicky, violent, or weird. (28)

Boykoff assumes that much of activism is aimed at garnering media attention so activists can raise awareness of an issue and generate public debate or discussion about that particular issue. The difficulty with garnering media attention is that the media thrives on spectacular events such that only the most creative, large, or outrageous displays by activists get media attention. Events that are outrageous and creative, however, are typically dismissed as weird and far from the lives of average citizens; and, even if they are covered in the media, they are not successful in convincing people to become part of that cause. This is a concern that applies to all four of the mothers in this book; any action that risks prison time, especially if it carries the risk of a felony conviction, will seem easily dismissible because few mothers will risk leaving their children in order to serve a prison sentence. Yet, what Boykoff fails to recognize is that the actions of Rush, Naar-Obed, Sheehan, and Wilson can be understood in another way. These mothers are not suggesting that their actions ought to be performed by all mothers, rather they act because they believe their actions are the right thing to do, whether or not the media notices, and they act so other mothers will be inspired to work for justice in their own way.

While popular media is structured in a way that prevents deep analysis of what these mothers are doing, academics can provide analysis of those acts that the media does not examine sufficiently. One of the most important contributions of academics is to provide critical analysis of the world; this analysis explains problems and injustices as well as the systems that cause and sustain the injustice. However, when academics focus on exclusively critical analysis of the world and its moral problems, that description can make it seem as though the world is inevitably unjust, and leaves no room to imagine what a just world could be. When academics focus on ideals and what a good society could be, then we have inspiration for what we could have if only we could resolve the injustice that we have today. Yet, critical analysis and articulations of what a just society would be still leaves us feeling helpless if we do not have a path from injustice to justice. The stories of Rush, Naar-Obed, Sheehan, and Wilson allow them and others to recognize injustice and to create justice in a concrete way.

The Role of Critique in Social Transformation

To say critiquing unjust institutions is one of the primary tasks of creating social change may seem to be an obvious point at first. Yet, the way in which a critique functions may be far less obvious than it initially seems. In its first instance, a critique can be as simple as an emotional response to a situation. Children critique their surroundings on a regular basis declaring, "That's not fair!" This statement can be used when children think a friend or sibling has more privileges than they do, whether they get to stay up later, or take a trip that the child wishes he could take. This statement can also be uttered by children when they are told that a favorite teacher has a serious illness such as cancer. Finally, I have heard my children say, "That's not fair!" in response to learning that because of the Iraq war, Iraqi children are suffering from more poverty, more sickness, and receiving less education than they suffered from before the Iraq War (Ismael 151–163). Each of these responses tells us something about the kinds of critique in which people can engage.

The first critique in which someone has something that a particular child wants for herself focuses the critique on the child as the center of attention. As far as instilling a sense of social justice or concern for others, this perception of "unfairness" leaves much to be desired, but does show some promise for instilling social justice if nurtured. The statement comes out of frustration with a circumstance in which the child can compare her situation to someone else's situation. In some cases, the charge that her situation is unfair may be completely incorrect when considered in a larger context. My six-year-old son might think it is unfair that his eleven-year-old sister gets to stay up until nine p.m. when he has to go to bed at eight p.m., but he does not have the perspective I have as a mother: younger children need more sleep, and he will be up earlier than his sister regardless of what time he goes to bed. In other cases, the awareness of unfairness is indicative of a larger social problem, as in Martin Luther King Jr.'s "Letter from Birmingham City Jail" describing why he will no longer wait for justice:

> . . . when you suddenly find your tongue twisted and your speech stammering as you seek to explain to your six-year-old daughter why she can't go to the public amusement park that has just been advertised on television, and see tears welling up in her little eyes when she is told that Funtown is closed to colored children, and see the depressing clouds of inferiority begin to form in her little mental sky, and see her begin to distort her little personality by unconsciously developing a bitterness toward white people. . . . (292–293)

As with the first example, a six-year-old child wants something another child has, but the larger context of the second example reveals a larger social problem. While in both examples an adult's perspective reveals whether there is an injustice happening, the child's ability to compare herself to another is an important part of ethical development that can be encouraged when she begins to feel empathy for people other than herself.

The second example I used in which children might state that something is unfair is the case in which a favorite teacher is suffering from cancer. Like the first example, the statement of unfairness is a direct result of the child's perspective on the situation. My daughter feels that this is unfair because she knows the teacher, the teacher is kind and generous, and she does not want her to suffer. This time the belief that the situation is unfair is on behalf of someone else since the child is not suffering, but someone else is. Yet, her statement of unfairness still needs to develop more fully for it to lead to a social critique since the teacher's sickness cannot be remedied by improved social conditions.

The third example I used of a child stating that it's unfair for Iraqi children to suffer as a direct result of war is a social critique, and it is precisely this kind of social critique that I will focus on in this book. Anyone who can make the statement, "That's not fair!" when confronted with the suffering of Iraqi children can then understand each of the previous examples in their larger social context as well. First, the child whose bedtime seemed unfair to him can step outside of himself to consider instead the plight of a child who cannot go to an amusement park because of the color of her skin. He can be told that the policy of the park is an arbitrary rule that should not be in place. Second, in the case of the sick teacher, we can teach the child that while her teacher's illness is unfortunate, we can only offer sympathy and comfort, and that no action can change the teacher's illness. Finally, in the third case we can begin to teach the child about the relationship between decisions in one country, the United States, and the effects elsewhere, Iraq.

Certainly, I am not suggesting a six-year-old will understand the complexities of social injustice; instead, I am suggesting that from an early age children have insight into injustice that can be reinforced and developed. I have drawn on three very different kinds of examples of injustice to demonstrate that recognition of social injustice can come from a variety of sources whether it is a personal comparison, empathy for people they know, or empathy for people like us but far away. The different examples also draw attention to the difference between situations we do not like and would change if we could, but are not an example of a social injustice. The distinction between an unfortunate event and social injustice will be important to maintain so we do not treat instances of injustice as though they are unfortunate events that cannot be helped. The intuition that something is not right must be unpacked in order to understand what precisely could be otherwise, if it could be changed, and how it could be changed.

The Role of the Ideal in Social Transformation

Once we discover and critique social injustice, one of the keys to social transformation for justice is to have some vision of what a just world would be. The history of philosophy is filled with descriptions of ideal societies; as far back as Plato, these descriptions depict a world in which people have all of the basic necessities met and can flourish because they also have access to goods beyond their basic needs. These visions give us a way to be *for* something positive and not just *against* something, and they help us to build our imaginative capacity so that the world as it is can be transformed into one in which everyone can flourish.

When feminists think about a just world for mothers and children, they have been instrumental in describing societies that value women and girls. Clearly, two of the features most important for protecting women and children are ridding the world of militarism and overcoming environmental destruction. In addition to being against militarism and environmental destruction, we need to envision a world that values mothers and daughters as much as fathers and sons. One of the leading theorists for these ideals is Luce Irigaray whose work began in the 1970s by critiquing patriarchal structures, and now focuses on describing how society can respect sexual difference and provide for the flourishing of females, which would in turn create a world in which both females and males can flourish.

In *Democracy Begins Between Two*, Irigaray lays out a political agenda that would guarantee natural and civil rights based on sexual difference (2001). The codes that she proposes would guarantee recognition of sexual difference within the law and within the family. For example, she proposes, "A relative destructuring of family unity, which requires that each man and woman should enjoy a specific civil identity which cannot be alienated in the family institution, a requirement which confirms the need for a new civil relationship between woman and man, women and men" (70). Certainly, her critique of family institutions as isolating for women has been accurate for many women as well as documented by many women including Simone de Beauvoir, Adrienne Rich, and Irigaray. But Irigaray's recommendation for destructuring family is unclear, especially in terms of how the relationships between woman and man, women and men, would change.

While Irigaray's suggestions for what precisely would change between men and women is not spelled out in detail, her suggestions for changing relationships between mothers and daughters provides an outline of how things might change to better support their relationships. These suggestions include changing the way mothers speak to their daughters by displaying images of mothers and daughters in homes and in public, using gendered pronouns and examples, and exchanging meaningful objects between each other (1993, 47–50). Her suggestions for flourishing relationships between mothers and daughters are part of her vision for a society that would not be hierarchical and demeaning for women and girls. Though she does not provide guidelines as to how this change could occur, she provides a description that can inspire the creative imagination. Even if we imagine a different kind of society than the one that Irigaray envisions, we can realize that society as it is, is not the only possibility. We can imagine living in a just world.

Perhaps one of the most inspiring aspects of Irigaray's philosophy is that she includes the natural world in her descriptions of an ethical society:

Such an objective [salvation of the earth] seems to me, today, to be the first one that we should pursue to ensure for each man and woman at least the right to life: to air, to water, to light, to the heat of the sun, to the nourishment of the earth. Rescuing the planet earth means, too, being concerned about happiness, as much for ourselves as for others. . . . What brings greater happiness than the return of spring? What is more marvelous than the lengthening of the days, than the earth once more covering itself in leaves and flowers and fruits? What is more joyful than the birds beginning to sing again? This happiness that we receive for nothing should be given priority protection by a politics which is concerned with the well-being of each and every one of us. (2004, 231)

This passage from Irigaray draws on the features of human life we want most for ourselves and for those we love. Rather than using the kind of narrow definition of "right to life" that only considers the life of a fetus, Irigaray looks instead at the very condition of possibility for all life. Whether it is human life, animal life, or vegetable life, all life needs air, water, light, the sun, and the earth. Yet, the basic needs that the environment fulfills do not go far enough in describing the happiness that is possible for humans, a happiness directly related to the earth itself. Certainly, those of us who have lived in places where winter can be harsh know how those first signs of spring—such as crocuses coming up through the snow—can renew the spirit, inspire hope, and bring happiness.

Irigaray's descriptions about protecting mothers and children, laws that respect sexual difference, and having a thriving environment are all inspiring and provide ample fodder for the creative imagination. Her work inspires her readers to participate in imagining a future based on happiness, love, and sexual difference. Her work describes a world in which people and the environment are regulated by love and sharing rather than economic exchange, which leads to militarism and environmental destruction (2008). Even so, her work provides few concrete details as to how we can transform the patriarchal societies she describes in her early work to societies that respect sexual difference described in her newest work.

The Role of Activists' Stories in Social Transformation

Social transformation is impossible without recognition that something is wrong with current institutions and relationships, and it is also impos-

sible without some vision of a society with just institutions and relationships. The gap between a society that is clearly unjust, especially for
mothers and children, and one that is peaceful and honors mothers and
children can seem so wide that people become overwhelmed by all the
personal and social changes that would have to take place. In the face
of this chasm, many people choose to simply continue with the status
quo in the hope that they can protect themselves and their families from
the worst injustice by staying silent even though they wish society were
different. Others continue with the status quo because they believe one
person cannot make a difference when injustice pervades every aspect
of society. The challenge, then, is to find a way to inspire people to act
on their ideals. This is why examples of activists with whom we can
identify can be a powerful source of social change.

In her work on activist mothering, Nancy A. Naples uses interviews and case studies of activist-mothers to research:

> the ways in which women from different low-income communi-
> ties in the United States come to identify and then challenge
> the relations of power that circumscribe their lives. What
> contributes to the process of politicization and what strate-
> gies are effective for fighting social and economic oppression
> at the local community level? Why do women of different
> racial, ethnic, class, cultural, and geographic backgrounds
> engage in these struggles, and what keeps certain women
> fighting despite minimal gains or even further devastation of
> their neighborhoods or towns? (1998a, 329)

The answer to this question seems to be that these mother-activists
develop their passion for justice and their perseverance not only by
virtue of how they are raised as individuals but also through the relationships that they develop with their communities (1998a, 329–333).
Through years of research about mothers from diverse backgrounds across
the United States, Naples uncovers the ways in which women take
issues and concerns about poverty, education, and discrimination out
of the private sphere and into the public sphere in order to achieve
political change. When oppression is effectively confined to the private
sphere, mothers remain isolated and struggle to support their families,
but not to change institutional structures. The significance of activist
mothers is that they bring their personal concerns into their community
work and their personal experiences become the impetus for political
change (1998b, 149–150). While Naples uses sociology to examine the

motivation for the activism of mothers engaged in the War on Poverty, this book focuses on the examples of four individual mothers working against U.S. militarism in order to dispel the myth that individuals cannot effect change against deeply ingrained institutional injustice; the myth that mothers' actions ought to be limited to the private sphere; and the myth that people should only act if they can guarantee their actions will have the desired results.

In order to further understand the purpose of examining the stories of how Rush, Naar-Obed, Sheehan, and Wilson became activists, I will turn to the work of Stanley Cavell. In *A Pitch of Philosophy: Autobiographical Exercises*, he focuses on the role of autobiography in philosophy, but his comments are helpful in thinking about the effectiveness of philosophy in analyzing activist stories as well (1994). Cavell provides insight into how individual experience points beyond itself. In particular, he states that, "[a philosophical education] is an education that prepares the recognition that we live lives simultaneously of absolute separateness and endless commonness of banality and sublimity" (vii). When we study moments from the particular story of an individual, those moments reveal both the separateness and commonness of every human life. The stories of Rush, Naar-Obed, Sheehan, and Wilson and their activism are stories that could not happen to any other person; even so, each mother's acts have significance for other women, mothers, and activists.

Cavell uses this same observation to make another point when he writes, "The philosophical dimension of autobiography is that the human is representative, say, imitative that each life is exemplary of all, a parable of each; that is humanity's commonness, which is internal to its endless denials of commonness" (11). While philosophy frequently has the reputation of being difficult and beyond the understanding of the average person, Cavell makes an argument for philosophy's role in revealing common experiences. The stories of Rush, Naar-Obed, Sheehan, and Wilson all provide examples of an individual person's capacity to challenge injustice and to provide examples of how the world could be a better place for all people.

Although many of Cavell's observations about autobiography apply to personal stories as well, the two differ in some important ways. Cavell begins his comments on autobiography in philosophy by reflecting on the arrogance for which philosophy is known, and he proceeds to list as examples Augustine, Kant, Nietzsche, Hume, Emerson, Thoreau, and Austin (3). Since all of his examples are men, it seems appropriate that a feminist analysis introduces women to the conversation and shifts the ground so we gain insight about humanity from others, not just from oneself. Another advantage of analyzing others' stories rather than using autobiography is that we are not caught in the difficulty of using "we" instead of "I" that Cavell describes: "Their basis is autobiographical, but they evidently take what they do and say to be representative or exemplary of the human condition as such" (8). When we study biography, the answer to why a philosopher would use "we" instead of "I" becomes clear since I (the philosopher) am studying someone else in order to gain insight into how the other person's actions inspire others and are aimed at others. The mothers in this book also create a "we" because their activism is not a solitary endeavor for their own benefit; their activism is inspired by relationship and aimed at relationship. Even when their actions are solitary and even when they face resistance from their communities and families, these women always have an awareness of the connections between all people and are part of a "we." Cavell overlooks the ways in which relationships can inform philosophy because he has only focused on purely abstract philosophy and the arrogance of autobiography, both of which are overcome by philosophical biography.

While Cavell analyzes autobiography for its philosophical significance, Keith Lehrer analyzes individual stories from a person's life for their significance to understanding the person. From Lehrer and Cavell, I want to emphasize that particular stories have significance beyond themselves. In "Stories, Exemplars, and Freedom," Lehrer offers other important insights into how life stories can provide examples that are useful for understanding beyond that particular story. He examines the purpose of using particular exemplars from a person's life in order to consider how those exemplars tell the story of one's life (Lehrer). Lehrer uses the theory of John Martin Fischer from Our Stories to argue that the story of one's life is made up of the actions of that person's life (Fischer), and while the story and the actual life may not always coincide, the exemplars are still significant for understanding how a person wants to represent herself or himself (Lehrer 1–17). His point is significant for this book since each of the women is described in numerous ways by numerous sources. Some people have described these women as "bad mothers," as "nutcases," and "dangerous." I will highlight the stories that reveal them as brave, visionary, and caring. The discrepancy between these descriptions comes from perspective. Those with negative perceptions have a stake in maintaining the status quo, while the perspective that I am advocating exposes the inequity of the status quo.

The concern for objectivity is also a focus for Genevieve Lloyd when she considers the purpose of autobiography in philosophy. She focuses on the autobiographies of St. Augustine, Jean-Jacques Rousseau, and Jean-Paul Sartre, she studies each of these biographies for their perspective on "relations between truth, time, and selfhood" (170), and she concludes that all of these fail to provide an objective account of a true self (184). Lloyd's concern that autobiography be objectively true neglects the reality that all stories about ourselves and others are shaped in their telling by the purpose of the telling and who tells the story. Nevertheless, Lloyd introduces an important consideration that I apply to my analysis of the narratives of the four mother-activists in this book. According to Lloyd, "An autobiography is as much the expression of a present self as it is the representation of a past one" (170). In the case of philosophical autobiography, the point of studying oneself as an object is to come to some sort of insight about an objective truth that is made visible by one's particular case. In the case of philosophical biography, the point of studying other people's narratives is to provide examples that can be applied to other situations and in other lives.

Chuanfei Chin provides another perspective that can help clarify why the stories of individual women can provide insight into larger cultural phenomenon. In her article, "Margins and Monsters: How Some Micro Cases Lead to Macro Claims," Chin draws several conclusions about how micro observations can apply to macro claims that will be helpful for understanding why case studies of women activists can tell us something about larger cultural issues for women and mothers, particularly issues related to building a culture of peace and nonviolence (341–357). Chin's study focuses on historical accounts of people at the margins of society and what those cases reveal about the majority of society. While she applies her analysis to historical studies, this analysis is applicable for other theoretical accounts of biography and memoir used to make larger claims about a society. In this book, I am using the examples of four mothers who engaged in nonviolent civil disobedience in order to reveal the ways in which U.S. policies and practices jeopardize children's well-being. Their examples also reveal the variety of peaceful means that mothers can use to oppose that violence.

One important way in which historians use micro cases, according to Chin, is to consider how the majority views those who are marginalized (341–357). The question of how Rush, Naar-Obed, Sheehan, and Wilson are viewed by the majority of society is an especially relevant question in my analysis since they are all marginalized by society as mothers who refuse to accept the status quo and want to expose the destruction and potential for destruction in U.S. society. For each of these women, the analysis of how they are viewed changes as a direct result of their civil disobedience. At times, people in society changed how they viewed an issue or changed their behavior. Rush, for example, describes a worker who, as a direct result of Rush's action, suddenly came to understand that he was helping to produce a nuclear weapon capable of terrible destruction. Wilson's repeated actions led a powerful chemical company to agree to zero-emissions at its new plant. At the same time that Rush and Wilson find success in changing how strangers perceive them, both suffer personal losses in their more intimate relationships. Rush describes her prison sentence as "being dead" to her children, and Wilson and her husband divorced as a direct result.

The second aspect I draw from Chin in my analysis of Rush, Naar-Obed, Sheehan, and Wilson is to analyze the interactions between those who are marginalized and the majority (341–357). The interactions between these mothers and the majority will be key to my analysis of the tension these mothers face between wanting the best possible society for their children and all children and the hardships for day-to-day mothering that their actions produce. The interactions that I will highlight will be between these mothers and the pressures the status quo puts on women in how they mother and the kind of children they are meant to raise, as well as between these mothers and the kinds of prison sentences and media attention they receive when they challenge the status quo by peacefully breaking laws.

While Chin wants to state the ways in which micro history can produce accurate macro claims about an historical period, my use of micro analysis has the aim of inciting critical analysis of the normative forces applied to mothering, the ways in which various practices of mothering can resist that normative force by critiquing institutions of injustice, and to provide inspiration for constructing alternatives to unjust practices and institutions. By using analyses of four mothers who challenge the U.S.'s culture of violence, I am drawing attention to the idea that each of these women is resisting a culture of war, which includes destruction of the environment. Sara Ruddick describes this culture in her article, "Making Connections Between Parenting and Peace":

> Feminists have been especially apt to recognize that military violence is not a distinct species isolated from other social practices. A continuum of harm, indifference, and willful injury

connects bedroom, boardroom, death row, and battlefield;
school room, university, welfare reductions, and precision-
guided bombs; racial profiling, racist employment practices,
and nuclear 'waste' in the lands of the poor. (207)

Ruddick's analysis in this passage reveals the spectrum of violence, which
guides my choice of subjects for this book. After listing the many forms
of injustice and violence, Ruddick states that children, "learn an elemen-
tary indifference to others' pain whether it is inflicted by 'advanced'
weapons or by illness, bad luck, social injustice, or domestic abuse" (207).
While her claim that children are indifferent to others' pain may be too
strong, she provides a list of the ways in which pain can be inflicted,
which indicates another way we can be overcome by the culture of violence surrounding us. If violence happens in every area of our lives and
happens as a result of practices seemingly beyond our control, how can
we ever hope to change this culture of violence to a culture of peace?

The answer to this question can be found through the examples
of activist mothers in this book. The first mother I study in this book is
Molly Rush whose action was aimed at disrupting the manufacture of a
nuclear weapon during the Cold War. Michele Naar-Obed, the mother
in Chapter 3, also destroys a nuclear warhead in her action a decade
later. Both women act as part of a community who are united in their
opposition to nuclear war, but they have very different support systems
for their children, which highlights the differences in circumstances that
mothers face when they decide to oppose militarism. While the first two
mothers act against militarism at times when the United States is not
at war, I will examine Cindy Sheehan's activism in Chapter 4 since she
became an activist as a result of the Iraq War and her activism focused
on ending the Iraq War. Finally, I conclude my case studies in Chapter
5 with an analysis of Diane Wilson whose activism began in response to
the violence perpetrated against Calhoun Bay where she was a shrimper.
That experience led her to actions on behalf of the environment, workers, and mothers across the globe.

The link between antimilitarism and concern for the environment
is a connection that demonstrates the ways in which U.S. women's
activism has historically recognized and resisted various forms of violence
that permeate society (Alonso). As Harriet Hyman Alonso describes in
her book, Peace as a Women's Issue: A History of the U.S. Movement for
World Peace and Women's Rights, the beginning of women's pacifist consciousness in the United States to the suffragists' struggle for the right

to vote. Today, she notes that women's pacifist consciousness expands to environmental consciousness as well (263).

Rush, Naar-Obed, Sheehan, and Wilson represent women from various economic backgrounds, regions of the United States, and cultural backgrounds; they bring an awareness of the ways in which violence permeates U.S. culture in different periods, during war and without war, and they provide inspiration on how to resist this militarization in order to move toward a peaceful society. Each of the women whose nonviolent civil disobedience is highlighted engages in the practice of calling attention to injustice and strengthening the elements necessary for a peaceful culture. These women's practices convey strength and compassion—characteristics of peace, rather than fear and isolation—characteristics of violence.

2

Choice and Consequences

Molly Rush

The Cold War era began in 1945 with negotiations to end the war in Europe and when the United States became the first country (and remains the only country) to use the atomic bomb against another country. This war continued until 1991 when the Soviet Union collapsed. Throughout this time, the use of nuclear weapons, the buildup of nuclear weapons, and the escalation in spending on military weapons became so deeply entrenched in U.S. culture that most people, even those directly involved in making the weapons, stopped thinking about the threat that these weapons pose and the culture of fear that these weapons produce (Chernoff; "US Arms Plan.").

The ways in which U.S. culture became militarized and opposition to this militarization began to appear in feminist theory in the 1980s. Of particular importance for this book is the essay "Morals, Mothers, and Militarism: Antimilitarism and Feminist Theory"; Micaela di Leonardo sketches the terrain of debates about maternity and militarism happening in the early 1980s (1985). Di Leonardo's essay is helpful in understanding the co-development of antimilitarism and feminist theory. She also helps to explain how feminists have grappled with the tension between understanding how the particular experiences of women shape their response to militarism and how these experiences can be applied in larger contexts. For mothers in the antimilitarism movement, the experience of maternity led them to activism against nuclear weapons and against the buildup of the military in society in general. The difficulty that di Leonardo exposes is that these mothers then apply their personal experience to all mothers, leading to essentialist descriptions of mothers and mothering. As feminists have long demonstrated and women have long experienced, women's lives and experiences are vastly different and their responses to wars, weapons, and militarism are also vastly different.

Because women have diverse experiences and responses and a single description of all mothers does not help to critique the militarization of U.S. culture, my focus in this chapter is on the response of a particular mother. Molly Rush, a mother of six children, had been involved with social justice issues through the Catholic Interracial Council in Pittsburgh, Pennsylvania since the early 1960s. As a result of her work on interracial rights, her commitment to the teachings of the Catholic Church, and her growing awareness of the harms that nuclear weapons cause, Rush became involved with a nonviolent Catholic group, Plowshares. On September 9, 1980, Rush acted to remind people of the threat these weapons pose and to remind people that we do not have to be part of the production of fear and violence implicit in producing nuclear weapons. As a result of their act, Rush was sentenced to a two-to-five-year prison term and five years on probation. She served 78 days of that sentence, and she successfully raised awareness of the threat of nuclear destruction, which will be elaborated in this chapter. Rush's nonviolent civil disobedience demonstrates the pressing ethical dilemmas that many mothers experience in the United States. She acted to disrupt the day-to-day militarism of U.S. society when she participated in a nonviolent action to make the nosecone of a nuclear weapon useless. Her actions were inspired by her experience as a mother who could empathize with all mothers, even those who do not share her perspective, but in carrying out her act she risked leaving her family and being unable to fulfill some of the maternal work that led her to act.

The Virtues of Maternal Work

In order to understand the conflict Rush feels between militarism and mothering, I will begin with an analysis of maternal practices as described by Sara Ruddick. Ruddick and I both recognize that men and women can carry out the practices she describes. Nevertheless, she describes them in *Maternal Thinking* as maternal because of the sociohistorical context; these practices are carried out by women more often than men and, even when men carry them out, U.S. society treats the practices as maternal practices (1995). It is also worth noting that in her later article, "Making Connections between Parenting and Peace," she discusses both mothers and fathers to describe those who nurture and care for children. She chooses these terms rather than the more generic term "parent" to point to the ways in which gender has an impact on parenting. Nevertheless, she continues to stress that the impact of gender should not reduce our understanding of parenting practices to gender stereotypes (213–214). Rush's maternal practices aimed at promoting peace exemplify many of the qualities that Ruddick describes.

In *Maternal Thinking: Toward a Politics of Peace*, Ruddick observes women's maternal practices in order to put forward a political theory that highlights the ways in which mothering can help guide action aimed at peace. According to Ruddick, "To be a 'mother' is to take upon oneself the responsibility for child care, making its work a regular and substantial part of one's working life" (17). In particular the demands of maternal practice include preservation of a child's life, growth of the child physically and mentally, and social acceptability. Each demand that Ruddick identifies builds on the previous demand. If the life of one's child is in danger, then it makes little sense for a mother to focus her energy on social acceptability. Thus, the urgency of creating a social environment in which children can be preserved and grow takes precedence to demands of social acceptability (17).

The reality of caring for the physical needs, the mental needs, and social acceptability is a lesson Rush learned at an early age. Rush, the oldest of eight children, grew up with a mother who loved her children and did her best to keep her family together in spite of an alcoholic husband who spent all of the family's money drinking (Norman 61; Aldridge et al. 370). The family's poverty was so extreme that at one point the children became wards of the Juvenile Court and were separated from each other and their parents (Norman 63). Throughout all of the hardship of her early years, Rush's mother held the family together with love and optimism. James, one of Rush's brothers, describes the attitude their mother lived by, "She looked forward to sunrise every morning and said her prayers every night that the sun would rise again for her in the morning. Didn't matter how bad she felt or how good she felt" (Norman 68).

While the physical deprivation caused suffering for all of the family, the descriptions of mental suffering and the hardship of social marginalization had an especially significant impact on Rush,

"As a teenager," said Molly, "I felt embarrassed and ashamed. It's so much worse having to apologize for your family, your father, his drinking. As a teenager, I just wanted to be like

everyone else. It was very painful, living in Mount Lebanon
[a wealthy suburb] until I was twelve and then having to get
Thanksgiving turkeys from the local parish." (Norman 64)

The descriptions that Rush and her brothers give of their childhood
paint a picture of a life in which the siblings came to rely on their mother
and one another in order to overcome the hardships of their life. The
lesson her siblings took from their early life was that mothers ought to
devote themselves to their home and their family above all else, which
would lead to conflict with Rush when she chose to become involved
in the Civil Rights movement and nonviolent civil disobedience against
the manufacturing of atomic weapons (Norman 68).

Yet, Rush cultivates another virtue that Ruddick identifies as an
aim of maternal practice: "respect for the independent, uncontrollable
will of the other" (73). Using Aristotle's approach to virtue in *Nichoma-
chean Ethics*, Ruddick identifies the ways in which this virtue can fail
through excess (domination) and defect (passivity). In seeking children's
preservation and growth, a mother must learn to appreciate her children
as different from herself even as she tries to guide them to flourishing.
But, discerning what flourishing will mean for a particular child requires
a difficult balancing act. A mother must rein in any tendency to domi-
nate and to exploit her power over her children. Children cannot flourish if they are simply conforming to roles that their mother enforces.
Yet, a mother cannot simply let her children guide themselves by being
absolutely passive. Children with a mother who takes no interest in their
development are unlikely to flourish. Flourishing will entail a process of
helping a child cultivate his or her unique qualities. As part of this process, the child's flourishing should be supported in his or her community
and in turn the child's flourishing should benefit the community. The
flourishing of the child and the community should be such that there is
reciprocity between what the child takes from the community and what
the child gives to his or her community (73).

Rush's respect for independence and cultivating one's particular
gifts for the sake of the common good is evident from her descriptions
of why she took part in nonviolent civil disobedience,

"Why me?" Molly wrote to her husband and her six children
on the lined stationery of the Berks County jail. It was the
question each member of her family asked over and over, "Why
her?" Molly had not begun as an activist, but she had grown

and evolved to the point that she could answer, "Because I know. Because I love you." Loving one's family members was not so unusual. *Knowing*, in 1980, was something else again. (Norman 234)

I will discuss the details of Rush's act that resulted in her arrest shortly, but for now I will focus on the relationship between the common good (loving one's family) and having a particular role in creating that good (communicating the uncommon knowledge Rush possesses). In 1980, it had been thirty-five years since the United States had dropped nuclear weapons on Hiroshima and Nagasaki, the country was not engaged in a war, and the military made a point of assembling each piece of a nuclear weapon in plants across the country so that no one place built a nuclear warhead and no particular workers felt as if they were building an atom bomb. But Rush was in a unique position to acquire knowledge of the threat of nuclear weapons. First, she had been active in civil rights activism and antimilitary activism since the early 1960s in Pittsburgh (Norman 234; Aldridge et al. 372; Faulk). Second, she had a religious commitment to nonviolence based on reading the Bible, reading the work of Thomas Merton (a Catholic monk who was an advocate of social justice and nonviolence), and her affiliation with the Plowshares community (a Catholic community of nonviolent activists who base their work on Isaiah 2:4: "They will beat their swords into plowshares and their spears into pruning hooks. Nation will not take up sword against nation, nor will they train for war anymore"). Through her work in social justice, Rush knew the threat posed by nuclear warheads and that the nosecones for these weapons were being produced nearby. Her religious commitments convinced her that she had a responsibility to act on her knowledge in order to protect her children and the community from that threat even if it meant they were opposed to her actions.

The link between children and their community is an important theme for Ruddick. She tells us that to provide for children's flourishing, "maternal care may extend as widely as the community on which growing children depend for their projects and affections" (81). In her account of protecting and nurturing children, Ruddick stresses the ways in which maternal thinking is necessarily concrete (93). Children cannot be raised in abstractly ideal conditions; rather, they encounter real circumstances of challenge and difficulty, just as their mothers encounter challenges and difficulty. Hence, effective mothering requires actions suitable to particular children in particular circumstances.

In many instances, a mother's particular burden is facing her community's judgments: "Beset by the difficulties of her work, the recalcitrance of her children, much inappropriate praise and blame, and the real limitations of her power, a mother is apt to become fearfully susceptible to the gaze of others" (111). In this passage, Ruddick chooses "gaze" to describe women's relationship to the society that praises and blames her. The gaze is an idea developed by Jean-Paul Sartre in *Being and Nothingness* when he tries to account for a subject's relationship to others. Sartre focuses on the experience of shame, especially with his powerful example of the subject who is caught peeking through the keyhole (340–400). In this example, a man is staring through a keyhole at something within a room when he suddenly hears a noise and is flooded with shame at the possibility of being discovered spying. Whether another person is there or not, the man is aware of himself as he would be viewed by another, and the relationship to this other person is marked by shame. Sartre's emphasis on shame in a person's relationships with others gives us an important insight as to why mothers can become "fearfully susceptible to the 'gaze' of others." A mother may fear that her actions will not measure up to the actions and expectations of others. Her children may seem more unruly, less intelligent, or less strong than other children. Because maternal work includes making children acceptable in society, any judgment against a mother's children is a judgment against a mother. In order to achieve judgments that will ease a mother's shame, she may become too willing to remain quiet and obedient even when she feels that her community's actions and values are harming her children.

Ruddick continues her use of Sartrean terms when she says that women are "inauthentic" when they replace conscience with submission (112). For these women, societal acceptance takes priority over their own concerns. Presumably, mothers are authentic when they recognize their situation in society and their responsibility for their own and their children's well-being. A mother's situation in society can be determined by many factors including sex, race, class, religion, marital status, and the number of children she has. In turn, her situation determines what actions are possible for her.

Ruddick's argument would benefit by turning to the work of Beauvoir rather than relying on Sartre. Beauvoir's book, *The Ethics of Ambiguity*, is more helpful than Sartre since the situation of a mother is replete with ambiguity and Beauvoir develops an ethics in which this ambiguity is sustained rather than clarified (1948). The ambiguity under consideration in this case is the conflict that mothers face when deciding whether they ought to confront the militarism that pervades society or to focus more locally on preparing their children to be part of this society, which is not likely to change. For Beauvoir, existentialism condemns oppression not from an abstract law that the subject follows, but because the subject who establishes the law can only find justification for her existence through the existence of others (72). While some might charge existentialists with egoism, Beauvoir argues, ". . . there is no ethics against which this charge, which immediately destroys itself, cannot be leveled; for how can I worry about what does not concern me? I concern others and they concern me. There we have an irreducible truth. The me-others relationship is as indissoluble as the subject-object relationship" (72).

Beauvoir's ethics is distinct even in existentialist philosophy. She maintains Sartre's insistence that the authentic person must act for her own freedom and take up her own projects, but for her the subject is always, already entwined with others. While Sartre's description of the subject's relationship to other subjects is most convincing when he describes shame, Beauvoir insists that the me-others relationship is indissoluble. People do not experience themselves and their projects as isolated from others' projects. She explicates the way in which the subject's ethical project always concerns the well-being of others. Because the self is always in relationship to others, Beauvoir avoids the difficulty of having to explain why the authentic person would be concerned with others' oppression. Every action has the potential that someone else will see what the mother does. When another sees the mother's action, that other can judge who the mother is and what she does. For Beauvoir, freedom consists in projecting oneself toward one's projects, and the freedom of the mother is never in conflict with working against the oppression of others. The authentic mother recognizes the obstacles in her society and works to overcome those obstacles, and every action carries the risk that someone else will see what she does. Thus, the authentic act takes the judgment of others into account, but also requires that she is ultimately the one who must choose what to do.

Once again, we can think about the various pressures that Rush faces as she decides that she will be part of an act of nonviolent civil disobedience. Throughout the interviews with Rush's husband, siblings, and children, it is clear that her family wanted her to stay home and not to risk imprisonment or a violent response to her nonviolent act. Her sister, Joanne, stressed the importance of staying home with her family by reminding Rush that it was their mother who kept their family

together through all of the hardships of their childhood (Norman 83).
After three of her brothers failed to talk her out of acting, her brother,
James, went to the FBI to expose Rush's plans, so they could prevent the
action from happening (Norman 84). Norman details the many times
that Rush's husband, Bill, tried to talk her out of her action. She quotes
him as saying, "It was stupid. Someone else should do it" (Norman 81).
Her oldest son, Dan, discourages her by saying, "Mother, I don't know
what I'd have done without you if I were Bob and Greg's age [14 and
12, respectively]" (Norman 102). Even family members who do not try
to talk Rush out of her action refrained from doing so because they
believed it would be impossible to change her mind not because they
supported her actions (Norman 103).

     As her immediate family pressures Rush to give up her intention to
pursue nonviolent disobedience, she consults with her religious community to discern what for her is the authentic and morally correct act. For
Rush, the two communities that are central to her ethical choices are her
family, who she wants to protect and to create conditions in which they
can flourish, and her religious community. Unfortunately, the judgments
of these two communities are in conflict, so much so that Bill compares
the retreats, prayer, and planning that happens between Rush and the
other Plowshares members to Marine training, "They separate you. They
say the same things over and over again. You're with the same people.
You go through the same things, go through suffering together" (Norman
82). Norman uses the words "Molly was in some kind of thrall . . . she
was in a state of psychic captivity . . . brainwashed" to describe Bill's
impression of the hold of the Plowshares members over Rush (Norman
82, 87, 89). Certainly, Rush's process of discernment, which included the
members of Plowshares but excluded her family, left her family feeling
frightened and confused about what Rush would be doing. Nevertheless,
as I will discuss shortly, her commitment to her family and to humanity
led her to a clear ethical choice: she must act to promote freedom and
to overcome fear (Norman 117; Aldridge et al. 370).

     When a mother is trying to determine what ethical acts she should
take up, she will find herself faced with many difficult decisions. As I
discussed above, the authentic person does not rely on abstract laws for
her ethical position; instead ethics is determined by concrete action.
The ethics of ambiguity requires concrete action both for one's own
freedom and against others' oppression, "But the others are separate,
even opposed, and the man of good will sees concrete and difficult

problems arising in his relations with them" (Beauvoir 73). Frequently, ethical engagement demands sacrifice. A mother may have to choose to sacrifice time with her own children in pursuit of creating a more ethical society for all children, or she may have to sacrifice actions that are aimed at the good of society for the sake of her children. Which sacrifice she should make cannot be predetermined in existentialist ethics; the choice is ambiguous and determined by particular mothers in concrete circumstances.

Ethical choices are ambiguous for Beauvoir, but they are not absurd. Ethics would be absurd if it were simply impossible to find meaning in our actions. Ethical choice is ambiguous because the meaning of an action is not predetermined; meaning is determined through action. Moreover, meaning is never definitively established; it must be reestablished constantly (129). Thus, a mother could authentically choose to sacrifice her activity on behalf of her own children or to sacrifice her efforts on behalf of her cause. The choice is authentic in as much as she is clear on why she is sacrificing one for the other and in as much as she is working for her own freedom and against the oppression of others.

In answer to the question, "Is existentialist ethics individualistic?" Beauvoir answers, "Yes" and "No." This ethics is individualistic because every individual has a particular, unique value; no one can be replaced by anyone else. It is also individualistic because each person lays the foundation for her own existence. Yet, this ethics is not individualistic in terms of considering the individual isolated from others. The subject's freedom is in relation to others and to the world; she assumes her freedom by rejecting oppression in any form and taking action in accordance with her own finitude, or her own limits and possibilities (156–159). That is, a mother recognizes her own situation and that she must work within that situation. Her options might be numerous; for example, she can choose many kinds of civil disobedience or many kinds of social activism. However, she cannot choose any action; for example, she cannot simply choose to eliminate all nuclear weapons. This kind of individualism is especially the case for mothers as described by Ruddick. According to Ruddick, a mother is concerned with her own place in society and her place cannot be separated from her children's place. Since society impacts how she raises her children and how she is judged as a mother, she must constantly assess whether her children are acceptable to others, whether society's values are ones she wants for her children, and how she will confront oppression when she finds it.

Militarism and Mothering

Women and mothers face many kinds of oppression depending on their personal circumstances and the country in which they live. The mothers who are most disadvantaged are mothers in developing nations who face disease, war, violence, famine, and poverty. By comparison, women in the United States have many advantages, yet the most disadvantaged women in the United States still face poverty, insufficient health care, insufficient educational opportunities, and violence. In this section, I will examine the ways in which U.S. militarism exploits the vulnerable and argue that while some mothers face more challenges than others, all mothers are affected by militarism.

The links between militarism and mothering are both a mainstay of many societies and a threat to the very actions that comprise mothering. In most societies, mothers are responsible for the care and upbringing of children. Mothers are responsible for their children's health, education, and assimilation into society, but support for militarism—which is a threat to their children—is expected. Moreover, many societies have gross discrepancies in the opportunities available for mothers and their children depending on race, class, and sexual orientation. The disadvantages of raising children when one is not white and wealthy are especially prevalent in the United States.

While wealthy mothers are able to shield their children from the military and are able to provide a college education without the help of scholarship programs offered by the military, low income and lower middle-class mothers are much more likely to have their children targeted by military recruiters. As the *Washington Post* reported in November, 2005,

> Many of today's recruits are financially strapped, with nearly half coming from lower-middle-class to poor households, according to new Pentagon data based on Zip codes and census estimates of mean household income. Nearly two-thirds of Army recruits in 2004 came from counties in which median household income is below the U.S. median. (Tyler)

Further analysis from The National Priorities Project analyzes recruitment data for the military and shows that the military is increasingly recruiting in low to middle income zip codes, while wealthy neighborhoods are under-represented ("National Priorities Project: Military Recruiting 2006."). In 2007, the Associated Press analyzed the U.S.

soldiers who had died in the war to that point and "found that nearly three quarters of those killed in Iraq came from towns where the per capita income was below the national average. More than half came from towns where the percentage of people living in poverty topped the national average" (Hefling).

Source after source documents the difficulty of recruiting since the Iraq War; the pressures of recruiting include the need for soldiers during war, keeping the army all-volunteer (which becomes a questionable claim if we consider that the military can keep people in the service beyond their initial enlistment), and people's reluctance to enlist during war. In an editorial that links concern for children's rights and health to military recruitment, Amy Hagopian and Kathy Barker critique the practice of military recruiting in high schools:

> The United States invaded Iraq in March 2003. Sustaining a war with an all-volunteer army is difficult, and military recruiters fell behind. If you're a military recruiter, where do you go to find prospects? Where do you find the mostly likely to enlist young people—those who may have limited incomes and are worried about affording college? In Seattle, recruiters head to the cafeterias at the lower-income central and south-end high schools (where young people on free and reduced lunch go to school). (20)

Each of these sources points to the disturbing reality that the U.S. military targets the working class and poor for their recruiting efforts. Even worse, the military actively recruits youth under the age of eighteen for military service. The military's practice of recruiting in high schools violates the United Nation's Convention on the Rights of the Child's Optional Protocol, which prohibits recruiting children under the age of eighteen (UN General Assembly). While the United States has signed the Convention, it is one of only two countries (Somalia is the other country) that has not ratified the convention (UN General Assembly). The UN website states that the delay in ratifying the Convention is due to the rigorous process of considering human rights treaties in the United States, but the long delay in ratification certainly does not signal a strong commitment to the rights of the child on the part of the U.S. government.

Another disturbing reality of the military is the recruiting that it does in minority communities. In "The Poverty Draft," Jorge Mariscal notes that the army has used the "Hispanic H2 Tour" and the "Takin' It to the Streets Tour" to promote positive images of the army in Hispanic and African-American communities in order to increase recruitment efforts (33). Once in the U.S. military, African-Americans and Hispanics are most likely to be in the lowest ranks despite increasing representation in the military in general (Segal and Segal 22–23).

The prevalence of low- and middle-class people in the military, and the disproportionate levels of minorities in the lowest ranks should signal a problem in the U.S. military. Even though poor and minority women's children are heavily recruited by the military, these women are expected to support U.S. militarism. Those with cultural influence promote the idea that having a child in the military should be a source of pride for mothers. On Mother's Day, 2007, U.S. President George W. Bush praised mothers for their role in supporting their children who are serving in the military,

> Mothers of military personnel provide support and encourage-
> ment while their sons and daughters defend our freedom in
> places far from home, and many mothers bring honor to the
> uniform of the United States while working to lay the founda-
> tions of peace for generations to come. (Proclamation 8140)

Bush's words to mothers reflect a common national belief that mothers ought to raise children who are willing to defend their country. The years that mothers invest in their children preserving their lives and helping them to thrive are risked for an abstract militarism. Bush's address is especially disturbing when we remember that Mother's Day began with mothers who were protesting World War I.

People are further manipulated when we are told that war will help to improve the lives of women in other countries (Zunes 14–18). When the United States began bombing Afghanistan in November, 2001, U.S. citizens were told that women's lives would improve in Afghanistan, but instead they faced increased violence: "While women are now allowed to go to school and leave the house unaccompanied by a close male rela-tive—rights denied to them under the Taliban—most women in large parts of Afghanistan are afraid to do so out of fear of kidnapping and rape" (Zunes 14). Prior to the Iraq War, many people believed that overthrowing Saddam Hussein would improve the lives of women in Iraq, but Human Rights Watch reports,

Many of the problems in addressing sexual violence and abduction against women and girls derive from the U.S.-led coalition forces and civilian administration's failure to provide public security in Baghdad. The public security vacuum in Baghdad has heightened the vulnerability of women and girls to sexual violence and abduction. The police force is considerably smaller and more poorly managed when compared to prior to the war. (Bjorken 1)

In spite of the insistence of people in power, mothers and their children are particularly vulnerable during war. These dangers include the threat of violence, lack of access to health care during pregnancy and childbirth, as well as a general lack of access to health care for their children (Kitzinger 232–233). A. Okasha, Professor and Director of World Health Organization Collaborating Center for Research and Training in Mental Health Institute of Psychiatry and the Past President of the World Psychiatric Association, details the effects of war on people living in a war zone. Among his conclusions,

Especially vulnerable groups include women, children, the disabled and the elderly. Loss and destruction of homes, loss of male heads of households to death or captivity, displacement and exposure to the dangers of sexual abuse and rape, almost always associated with *war* crimes leaves women, especially *mothers* at high risk of hopelessness and depression. The level of depressive symptomatology in the mother was found to be the best predictor of her child's reported morbidity. (Okasha 199)

All of these reports on war's effects on women emphasize the ways in which war disrupts traditional roles that women play in many societies. These roles make them dependent on men and responsible for the care of children, the disabled, and the elderly. War, though, destabilizes the structures that make women's care of others possible, which in turn destabilizes the society itself.

The challenge, then, is for mothers to resist the ideology of people in power. Many mothers are skilled at finding ways to preserve their children and to nurture their children even in the most difficult of situations. Some mothers are subjected to sexual and racial discrimination, poverty, or discrimination based on sexual orientation. These mothers may not have the reserves necessary to protest against militarism. Other U.S mothers are among a privileged class of people; they are financially stable, white, and their children are healthy. These women have an opportunity to empathize with mothers who suffer from poverty, racism, and the effects of war. Moreover, these women are in a special position from which they can act on behalf of other mothers. Instead of staying quietly under the radar, Molly Rush uses her social position to call attention to the costs of war.

Confronting Militarism

In order to understand how mothers can call attention to the costs of war, we can turn to Chantal Mouffe's explanation of the way in which a nation's identity is tied to a distinction between friend and enemy. Once a group is labeled "enemy," then fear is created in the friend group, which allows people in the friend group to justify actions against the enemy that would not be tolerated in one's own group. In the current context the enemy is the "terrorist" against which the United States and its allies must mobilize. In Rush's sociopolitical context the enemy is the "communist" against which the United States must mobilize. The mission for mothers who engage in civil disobedience is to challenge the distinction between friend and enemy and to show that the costs of war are borne by people on both sides of a conflict.

As Mouffe explains in The Return of the Political, Western society has undergone a profound change in identity between the 1980s and today (Mouffe 1993). Mouffe traces this identity shift, "to the collapse of Communism and the disappearance of the democracy/totalitarianism opposition, that since the Second World War, had provided the main political frontier enabling discrimination between friend and enemy" (3). From 1945 through 1991, American identity depended on being democratic, which meant not being communist. Other democracies were viewed as friends, communists were viewed as the enemy, and countries associated with neither were the battleground. During this time, the United States and the Soviet Union engaged in amassing weapons as a method of deterrence.

According to Mouffe's analysis, the United States faced an identity vacuum when the Soviet Union collapsed in 1991. U.S. identity needs more than being a democracy to understand itself. U.S. identity requires understanding itself as what it is not; in 1980, the United States is not communist. September 11, 2001 provided an opportunity for the United States to find a new enemy: terrorism. North America is democratic, not terrorist, and American military power has, since 9/11, been used to uphold and defend this distinction. Thus, a mother who wants to speak out against militarism can work to undermine the notion that identity is determined by what we are not and instead focus on the ways in which people and nations are necessarily connected. Each of the mothers in this book is a powerful example of mothers who work to undermine the friend/enemy distinction. Here, we are considering Rush's protest against the U.S. nuclear weapons program in 1980, and the protest's effects on others, which allows us to understand Rush as a precursor to the other mothers in this book (Norman 1989).

Rush would seem to be the ideal woman to whom U.S. political leaders can sell militarism. She is the mother of six children, part of a white, heterosexual, working-class family. From Pentagon statistics that have been analyzed by the National Priorities Project, her children are the most likely to be recruited for the military. Today, Rush would be part of the target audience for rhetoric which insists that women in Iraq and Afghanistan will be safer and have more freedom if U.S.-led forces occupy their countries. Yet, Rush recognized that the rhetoric of security during the Cold War was false. As cited by Norman, Rush recognized that, "Her children's lives were linked to the lives of the enemies' children. Hers could not survive unless theirs could too. To love one's enemy, the New Testament elucidation of the Old Testament absolute was newly the condition of survival" (44). In this passage, Rush affirms the indissolubility of the me-others relationship that Beauvoir discusses. Loving one's enemy is not distinct from loving oneself and one's children. Rush successfully uses her social position—her race, class, and heterosexuality—to disturb assumptions about what mothers can do to protect children from the dangers of war by refusing to act in accordance with those assumptions as if they were imperatives.

Rush's insight into the connection between her children's lives and the lives of the enemies' children takes on an urgency to act to preserve all children's lives, and she—along with seven others—decided to engage in nonviolent civil disobedience to draw attention to the destructiveness of nuclear weapons, to expose the vulnerability of power, and to call others to responsibility. On September 9, 1980, the Plowshares Eight, a group of nonviolent practitioners of civil disobedience, entered General Electric (GE) Nuclear Missiles Re-entry Division in King of Prussia, Pennsylvania. That day two of the Plowshares Eight entered Building

Number 9 and gave literature to Robert Cox, the guard on duty, about Plowshares and told the man that they were there peacefully and non-violently. As Cox tried to call his boss to report the protestors, the two prevented him from calling: Cox claims he was forcefully prevented from calling; the activists described a less violent scuffle. Meanwhile, the other six members entered Building Number Nine, and all eight proceeded into the building (24–25). There, they hammered the nose cones of two Mark 12A warheads, poured blood on documents and prayed for peace (26–28). The nosepiece that they were targeting would eventually end up as part of a warhead with a thermonuclear bomb of at least 350 kilotons—twenty-eight times more powerful than the atomic bomb dropped on Hiroshima (36–39).

When Rush planned her action, she expected her act to be largely symbolic. She expected that their hammers would be symbols of beating swords into plows, the Biblical verse upon which the group had been founded, but she did not believe she would be able to actually damage the nose cone. Much to her surprise, she was able to damage the weapon, "That a small woman, only five feet two inches tall, hammering with an ordinary household hammer, could render these two war heads forever useless, 'exploded so many myths in my mind!'" (38). In another interview thirty years later, Rush continues to remember the moment of discovering the vulnerability of these weapons with astonishment, "I thought, these things are as vulnerable as we are, and we can undo what has been done. That was an amazing moment" (Brown and Muller). The weapons are not indestructible; they are made by human hands and are vulnerable to human tools.

Not only are the weapons themselves vulnerable, the powers that allow these weapons to be made are also vulnerable. Rush and the Plowshares Eight seemed to be a relatively harmless group: a mother, two priests, one former priest, a peace community member, a musician and retired college teacher, a nun, and a lawyer. But, Rush and her co-defendants quickly discovered the seriousness of their actions when they were charged with crimes that carried a possible total sentence of sixty-four years in jail, which would have made her 108 at the end of her prison term (32–33). In fact, authorities take civil disobedience by ordinary citizens very seriously because of its capacity to disrupt a society's balance of power:

> For many, Molly's action illuminated both the intransigence
> of institutions addicted to warfare and their fragility. The

arms race could go forward only with massive cooperation and consent. The Plowshares Eight provided an instance in which citizens withdrew their consent. That instance was fraught with possibilities. (Norman 220)

U.S. society depends on cooperation from people in order to function. Our police forces and National Guard are there to identify isolated instances of noncooperation and noncompliance. They rely on the threat of public prosecution and hearings to prevent people from acting in the first place (Boykoff 61–77). By deliberately hammering the nosecone of a nuclear weapon and accepting the consequences of the act, Rush and the other Plowshares activists refused to allow the threat of arrest, trial, and imprisonment to intimidate them. If everyone refuses to cooperate with a law or way of acting, then the authorities are powerless to enforce every law. When the Plowshares Eight walked into the GE plant in King of Prussia, they exposed that the security for this nuclear warhead-making facility relies on people not walking in; no one prevented them from entering the facility, hammering the nose cones, or spilling their blood.

The Plowshares Eight also exposed the voluntary cooperation of those who work in the facility to produce these nose cones. Instead of being able to go to work in a pristine environment in which vitamins are as likely to be made as pieces of nuclear warheads, that day the workers had to confront the fact that they help make weapons that can destroy millions of "soft targets" (civilians who are the unintended victims) and the infrastructure (roads, bridges, schools, hospitals, libraries, museums) of an entire society (37). Prior to that September morning, the workers seemed to know very little about what they were manufacturing, preferring to think only of their work as a job that could provide for their families rather than a job that produced nuclear weapons (34–35). But on that day, the workers of Building Number 9 faced the reality of what they produced.

When Ruddick discusses the impact of society's gaze on a mother, she emphasizes the vulnerability and coercive force that the gaze can have on a mother (111). The Plowshares Eight, though, reveal that the gaze can also emphasize people's ethical responsibility. Until the Plowshares Eight entered Building Number 9, the people working there were able to maintain their position and image of themselves as isolated workers doing a job that affected no one but themselves and their coworkers. They could maintain a perception of themselves as good, caring people because their reference was self-defined. For those workers who knew they were building part of a nuclear weapon, they could also tell themselves that they were doing good, patriotic work that would protect other U.S. citizens. Each person did her job well, so that the next person could do his job well. When the Plowshares Eight acted, they exposed the workers of Building Number 9 to an external gaze, a gaze that calls each worker into question. The work at GE was exposed in its connection to making nuclear weapons, an activity that is neither good nor caring. The people subjected to the gaze of the Plowshares Eight then had an opportunity to explain their actions to those who gazed at them.

While Rush was successful in exposing the vulnerability of weapons and power and subjecting those who participate in manufacturing nuclear weapons to an external gaze, she also had to sacrifice some of what led her to her action in the first place: her own children and her role as their mother. At the time of the action, Rush's six children were between the ages of twenty-five and twelve. Some of her children were already married and living on their own, but the youngest children still relied on their mother, and Rush, quoted by Norman, agonized over the possibility that she would be gone while they grew up, " 'Today I feel my death to all that in its fullest, sledgehammer reality,' says her notebook. 'I saw the boys grow tall, begin to shave, remembering me with fondness, occasional visits or notes, and, perhaps, resentment' " (45–46).

Rush spent a total of seventy-eight days in jail; far fewer than the sixty-four years she could have spent if convicted of every charge and sentenced to the maximum penalty. When examining the cost of civil disobedience, however, we cannot skip to the end result to reassure ourselves that no one was harmed. We must instead consider the agony of deciding between two wretched alternatives: standing by and saying nothing against a government whose nuclear pursuits risks the lives of her own children and children everywhere; or, engaging in civil disobedience to protect her own children and children everywhere such that she will "be left out of their everyday reality" (46).

If we could be absolutely dispassionate and assess the dangers of nuclear weapons and the dangers that they pose to children, then we can easily justify Rush's actions. Rush should act because she could save millions of lives; whereas mothering her particular children only directly benefits six people. The weapons being made in King of Prussia could destroy 293 square miles, as compared to three square miles destroyed by the Hiroshima bomb (Norman 37). Even if the MX Mark 12A hits its target with flawless precision, 293 miles will be destroyed along with the target, miles that almost certainly contain schools, libraries, hospitals, homes, and civilians. Thus, Rush's action had the potential to destroy a bomb that could kill hundreds of thousands of people, as well as injuring and sickening many, many more. Her action also had the potential to stop people from being unknowingly complicit in potential destruction. In this case, we might stand back and say that Rush's action is perfectly rational because depriving six children of their mother (even if it would have been permanent) is worth saving untold numbers of other adults and children. One woman wrote in support of Rush's commitment to her own and others' children, "Molly Rush is trying to protect her children and everybody's children and grandchildren, from such a horrendous possibility [nuclear destruction]" (50).

This simple calculus, though, overlooks the responsibility that women have for their particular children, a claim that seems to be accurate for many women who have invested time in raising their children. As Rush raised her children, she took particular care for their well-being; she did not care for all children as she did her own. Ellison's interviews with Rush's children reveal a mother committed to social justice work, but also a woman who took care of the house, the kids, the meals, and her husband. Rush was a woman devoted to her family and their well-being. She was not disconnected from their well-being in the way that other activists' children have described their parents (Gandhi, for example, who was infamously estranged from his oldest son). Rush had been preparing her children for her absence by explaining that she was acting for them and for every child, "The children were torn between admiration for her intervention, which they understood to have been on their behalf, and their wish that their mother could continue as she had been, working, cooking, spending time with them" (103).

Of course, Rush did decide that as a mother she needed to act and would do so through civil disobedience: hammering nuclear warheads and spilling her blood on the plans for the warhead. Her participation came directly from her love for her children and their trust in her: "What does it mean to trust a parent?' Molly wondered. 'How does one love one's children?'" (107). She determined that one of her primary duties as a mother is to protect her children's lives and to take the steps that she can to prevent unnecessary death: "When someone accepts nuclear war, she breaks a trust, because it is accepting passively a death that can be prevented—accepting death for oneself and also for those one loves" (107). Rush's words emphasize the importance of preserving a child's life, part of the primary work of mothering identified by Ruddick.

The key to understanding Rush's decision to participate in civil disobedience is that her deep love for her children and their well-being allowed her to empathize with all mothers and parents who try to protect their children every day. She saw pictures of the damage done by the atomic bomb at Hiroshima and read accounts from survivors about how mothers fruitlessly tried to save children. As she read the accounts and saw the pictures, Rush made the connection between those victims and her own family. She could have been the mother searching for a missing child, her daughter could be the mother clutching the charred remains of her newborn baby, and her sons could be the children left without a mother (106–107).

Not only did she see the connection between her family and their survival and the survival of enemies' families, Rush also saw the connection between those who would use nuclear weapons, those who produce nuclear weapons, and those who remain silent about the production and use of nuclear weapons. All of these people are complicit in building a culture of death rather than a culture of life. "'Everyday, many people go to work, building these weapons that are going to kill their children and my kids,' she said, wonder in her voice" (38). During the trial, it became clear that the workers at the GE plant maintained a disconnection from their work and most claimed they did not know what they were manufacturing. Instead of focusing on what they were producing, the workers focused on the complexity and challenge of their jobs and the paychecks and health insurance that the jobs provided for their families. As a result of the Plowshares Eight's action, at least one engineer resigned his position, since he could no longer disconnect from what he was manufacturing (170–209).

Many of the rest of us remain silent about nuclear weapons because we believe "the myth of security" and "the myth of powerlessness." The myth of security tells us that stockpiling nuclear weapons will discourage others from using any sort of weapons against the United States if only we have the most weapons and the most powerful weapons. The myth of powerlessness cultivates the belief that we are powerless against the decisions of our government; that if they decide to build up our nuclear stockpile, then we can only hope that they will never use it. Thus, the value of civil disobedience is not measured by the act's ability to stop all manufacturing of nuclear weapons, but by refusing to accept the myths of ideology. For Rush, one of her commitments is a commitment to mothering and in order to do that effectively, she finds a way to do everything that she could do to protect her children and to protect other children:

"I could have closed my eyes and hoped for the best," she wrote, and many would have been far happier had she done that. "But that hope would have been a blind hope based on refusal to see and refusal to act responsibly." On September 9, 1980, "I felt very clear that I had brought my concerns for my kids' lives and my hope in the future and my love of being a peace-maker all together. When we walked into that G.E. plant, I felt no fear. I felt tremendous peace. [That act] freed me from the myth of my own powerlessness. I didn't end the arms race, but I certainly acted on behalf of life. And I certainly acted in a way that connected with a lot of people." (Norman 229–230)

Civil disobedience is about acting on behalf of principles that are higher than the available laws. It disrupts the standard order and day-to-day activities of a society. Sometimes, it wakes up a society to a new reality, as witnessed through Martin Luther King, Jr. and Mohandas Gandhi. Sometimes, society persists in believing its myths of security and powerlessness. Rush, though, stresses that disrupting these myths brings freedom and hope (Aldridge et al. 370). The authentic person to whom Ruddick and Beauvoir appeal reveals the many ways in which mothers support U.S. militarism, as well as revealing the possibility that each of us has ways in which we can withdraw our support.

Successful Protests

Ultimately, Rush is successful in her protest because she uses the privileges of her race, class, and heterosexuality to challenge the militarism of U.S. society. We might expect a working-class mother to encourage her children to join the military in order to have career opportunities and education opportunities that her income cannot provide. As a product of U.S. society, Rush is expected at the very least to support the country's insistence that she and her children are safer if they are shielded by nuclear weapons.

The period in which she protested against nuclear weapons marked a period in which women and feminists were coming together with a sense of urgency to work against the threat of nuclear weapons. *Over Our Dead Bodies: Women Against the Bomb*, from 1983, collects the work of many feminists from this time who from a variety of perspectives voice their sorrow over the effects of the atom bombs dropped on Hiroshima and Nagasaki, their concern about the build-up of nuclear weapons, and their fear for children and others who could become the next victims of nuclear warfare (Thompson). Of particular importance in this volume is the contributors' efforts to expose the myth that a stockpile of nuclear weapons makes us safe. Exposing these myths is the central concern of essays by Beryl Ruehl, who exposes the myth of safety by balancing the threat of nuclear annihilation between the United States and the former-USSR; Suzanne Wood, who exposes the illusion of protection provided by nuclear weapons; and Dorothy Thompson, who exposes the myth of security. The temptation to believe these myths is described by Jeannette Buirski, in her article "How I Learned to Start Worrying and to Hate the Bomb: The Effects of Nuclear Bombardment,"

> There are certain myths concerning nuclear war to one or all of which the vast majority of us subscribe: they enable us to live a life of relative unconcern in the face of probable annihilation. (15)

In the 1980s, the dominant myth that feminists were fighting was the myth that the threat of mutual destruction would prevent nuclear war and keep all of us safe. In our own era, mothers are expected to believe that the U.S.-led war and occupation in Iraq and Afghanistan are for the benefit of the women and children of those countries.

Rush's example of shattering myths can open a window through which others can see that the well-being of U.S. children is linked to the well-being of all children, and every person's safety is threatened by the production of violence. Rush's actions in 1980 continued the tradition begun in 1953 when U.S. women first used their status as mothers to draw attention to the threat posed by nuclear weapons and to debunk the myth that nuclear weapons provide security (Alonso). Rush's actions provide a model for women and mothers who want to challenge social injustice that threatens not only their children, but all children. While she found a community with whom she could act, her nuclear family did not provide support for her action and she had to make a choice between only mothering her children and including her children's well-being with the well-being of every child, which felt to her like abandoning her own children. Her fearlessness in confronting injustice and exposing the danger of nuclear weapons and militarism challenge the view that mothers' work is in the private sphere, and also points to the need to rethink models in which mothering should happen only within a nuclear family. In the following chapter, Michele Naar-Obed's practice of mothering as part of a community provides an example in which the model of mothering and action is transformed.

3
_____

The Power of Horizontal Support

Michele Naar-Obed

The significance of mothering has been the subject of countless narratives, short stories, and poetry. The dominant theme of many of these accounts of mothering is that a woman's identity becomes subordinate to her children and she loses her independence. For some, becoming a mother is the fulfillment of childhood dreams and social expectations. For others, becoming a mother is suffocating and cuts women off from their identity. Molly Rush's experience of mothering inspired her to act on behalf of her children and every mother's children, but when she acted, she felt as though she had died to her children and that they were left motherless while she served time in prison.

An alternate possibility is that mothering in some contexts can be a continuation of a woman's identity rather than a new identity. Michele Naar-Obed is a woman whose transformation into a mother connected her more deeply to her community and to the world. Because of this connection, she was able to leave her 23-month-old daughter in the care of her community and disarm a fast attack nuclear submarine, a felony act, which she knew would result in a prison sentence. She was successful in calling people's attention to the presence of nuclear weapons in their midst, creating dialogue about the threat of nuclear weapons, and in creating a way of mothering that allowed her and her daughter to be supported while she served time in prison. I will discuss Naar-Obed's narrative about maternity and nonviolence because she is an exception to many of our society's common beliefs: she gave up a lucrative job to live simply in community; she and her partner chose to have a child as part of that community rather than to become a separate nuclear family; and she chose to break the law and serve time in prison to emphasize her interdependence with other mothers and their children. I will use Luce Irigaray's discussions

49

of cultivating intersubjectivity and maternity (1996; 2001; 2002) to argue that Naar-Obed's mothering offers a prophetic alternative to the binaries and restrictions that other feminist writers take for granted.

Isolated Mothering

In "Oi Mother, Keep Ye' Hair On! Impossible Transformations of Maternal Subjectivity," Lisa Baraitser contrasts woman prior to maternity as an "earlier independent, solitary, unitary self" with woman as mother who is "something messy, interdependent, and altogether more blurred" (218). She notes that in many popular accounts of motherhood women look back with longing at the woman who was in control of her life and her projects, and as mothers these same women feel the weight of failure, choosing between their prior selves and their children (220). Baraitser's own description of becoming a mother, what she calls "mother-writing," reveals a grief that overwhelms her experience of becoming a mother. She writes:

> Motherhood is the pitilessness of the present tense . . . In this immediacy, I am brought face to face with the patched over, broken bits of myself, the cracks in relations with mother, lover, siblings, friends. Everything is challenged, like in analysis, painfully peeled back . . . in the grip of a mute and helpless grief . . . I know that everything has changed. I am unsteady, dizzy, like I'm relearning to walk after a long illness. I imagine a war has taken place while I've been away . . . Severed from myself, like the cut end of a worm, I am disorganized, stunned. (228)

In Baraitser's writing, woman and mother replaces the dyad masculine and feminine. As the feminine is unknowable, chaotic, and shrouded in mystery for the masculine, so is the mother for the woman. The mother is cracked, mute, helpless, and foreign; whereas, woman is a coherent unity. The prevalence of grief, regret, and longing lead Baraitser to reject the notion that becoming a mother is transformative, and she turns to the work of Irigaray to provide a basis for a mimetic appropriation of motherhood. Just as sixteenth-century Jewish women found a way to express their sexuality by donning another's hair, Baraitser suggests that through mimesis a mother might find liberation from her bondage to the child (235–237).

What strikes me in Baraitser's mother-writing—both her own and that of others whom she cites—is that these women are quite solitary in their maternal experiences. Naar-Obed's experience of mothering provides another scenario in which a woman's transition to motherhood is not experienced as an isolated event, but rather as an entry into a transformed community and transformed interdependence. Interdependence is a traumatic event in Baraitser's analysis because it marks the end of a solitary self who is free from "the coarseness of its own material effects" (227). In this analysis, woman becomes the masculine of a traditional masculine-feminine binary. Yet, the substitution of woman for masculine is deeply problematic if Irigaray's theory is the theoretical base. Rather than figuring woman as a masculine subject, a woman who is interdependent can continue this interdependence as a mother.

The narrative evidence that Baraitser provides certainly indicates that many, if not most women probably experience profound loss when they become mothers, but it is possible that women can also experience a positive transformation if they have cultivated an interdependent subjectivity rather than modeling their subjectivity after masculine ideals. For Irigaray, the stress on independence "is a denial, an annulment of these intersubjective relationships which, from infancy, have marked [the body]" (2001, 32). No one begins as an isolated being in the world: "In my present body I am already intention toward the other, intention between myself and the other, beginning in genealogy" (32). Genealogy marks every woman and every man even if a particular mother and father are not adequate. The relationship to the parents is always present even if they were neglectful or harmful. The relationship to the parents marks every person such that living without denial means accepting oneself as intersubjective. The reality of intersubjectivity does not mean that women have to naively or submissively accept the status quo or an inferior position in relation to men. For Irigaray, cultivating the relationship of intersubjectivity means creating a horizontal relationship in which difference is emphasized without hierarchy. Cultivating subjectivity can lead to building communities that support each member as well as larger transformative projects.

Intersubjectivity

Prior to discussing the role of maternity in Irigaray, we must first turn to Irigaray's description of a woman's subjectivity developed through her relationships with others. For Irigaray, subjectivity should not be the sort of individual endeavor that Baraitser describes. Instead, subjectivity develops through vertical and horizontal relationships with other women and with men. Any individual woman's subjectivity is irreducible to any other woman's subjectivity, but her subjectivity is intertwined with others' subjectivity and is always intersubjective. The intersubjectivity that Irigaray prescribes allows for space between individuals and a return to the self, both of which provide protection against hierarchical and submissive relationships.

While many philosophical theories of subjectivity treat the subject as an isolated individual, Irigaray begins with the observation that the subject is always, already in relationships with other people. One of the first forms of relationality a person will experience is a vertical relationship. The vertical relationship has three forms in Irigaray's writing: person in relation to the divine, person in relation to her/his genealogy, and the person in relation to her/his teacher or student(s). Although a vertical relationship seems to indicate a hierarchy between subjects, verticality is better understood as a temporal relation as well as a relation in which wisdom is transmitted.

When Irigaray writes about the ideal relationship between student and teacher, she describes teaching as opening up oneself to welcome the other. The teacher, in this perspective, teaches a subject according to her/his own knowledge and knowledge of the student. This perspective emphasizes the relationship between knowledge and the subjects rather than positing teaching as the transmission of purely objective material. A teacher who tries to transmit purely objective material fails to recognize the irreducible difference between the teacher and the student. Irigaray's conception of teaching emphasizes the otherness of the student. The vertical relation between student and teacher nurtures the unique development of the student instead of trying to make the student a replica of the teacher. This perspective on verticality characterizes each of the vertical relationships, which will be evident as I discuss the relationship between Naar-Obed and the divine, and Naar-Obed and her daughter.

Another important type of relationship for Irigaray is the horizontal relationship: the relationship of people of the same sex amongst themselves and the relationship between the sexes. Vertical relationships and horizontal relationships occur together. A woman has a vertical relationship with her mother by virtue of their genealogy, and they have a horizontal relationship by virtue of their sex. The emphasis in the horizontal relationship is on difference, equality, and reciprocity.

Even in the horizontal relationship of two people who are the same sex—female, for example—difference is important because women are not reducible to a single, static definition. Instead, sex is continually defined by those who are that sex. The definition of being a woman is fluid and dynamic.

Naar-Obed's vertical and horizontal relationships allow us to understand why she chose to participate in a nonviolent direct action against the U.S.'s nuclear buildup, an action that risked an extended absence from her daughter. The vertical relationships that influence Naar-Obed are her relationships with God and with her daughter. I will discuss the relationship with her daughter in the following section. Here, I will describe Naar-Obed's account of her nonviolent direct action, and her emphasis in this account on her relationship with God. This relationship allows her to discern a moral path and to create relationships with other people that help her to pursue this path. For her, God does not require converting other people to her faith; rather, God requires that she work to secure human flourishing, to fight against forces that undermine human dignity.

Naar-Obed's relationship with God led her to become part of a community that intentionally lives according to God's prescriptions. This community—Jonah House—lives according to a biblical passage: "The plowshare witness is an attempt to bring Isaiah's vision (Isaiah 2:4) to life. It envisions a time when all of God's people come together to live on the Holy Mountain to live as sisters and brothers" (Naar-Obed 8). The Isaiah passage by which Jonah House lives states that God's people, "shall beat their swords into plowshares, and their spears into pruning hooks: nation shall not lift up sword against nation, neither shall they learn war any more." Within Jonah House, the people understand nuclear weapons as the greatest threat to people living together in peace. They also believe that God intends the kingdom of heaven to be lived in this world. Naar-Obed and her community share a particular interpretation of Christianity that emphasizes interconnection between people and living peacefully together.

While she grants other interpretations are possible, Naar-Obed's interpretation does not lead to the conclusion that every interpretation is correct. While the Bible allows for multiple interpretations, some can be wrong. For instance, an interpretation may be wrong because it misunderstands or mistranslates passages. The vertical relationship between Naar-Obed and the divine is particular to her and her community, but she is not solely responsible for the interpretation of the biblical passage she lives by. The interpretation is transmitted from outside of her. The community receives the Bible as God's teaching, and they interpret that teaching according to their particular context.

The vertical relationship between Naar-Obed and the divine is directly related to the horizontal relationships in her life. The relationships that contextualize Naar-Obed's nonviolent direct action are her relationships to Jonah House, to her husband, and to the world community. In 1992, Naar-Obed became a member of Jonah House. This house joins together people from all walks of life and various commitments to marriage and celibacy. The members unite to live according to the Biblical imperative of working for peace. She describes her decision to join the community as arising from the political activism in which she had been engaged. Since 1991, Naar-Obed had been participating in minor nonviolent direct actions that resulted in, at most, a five-day jail sentence. In 1992, though, she was considering a direct action that would be interpreted as a felony in the judicial system. She knew that this action would be severely disruptive to the doctor, the other staff, and the patients with whom she was working at the time. Without her job, however, she would have no way to support herself. As a result, she researched Jonah House and decided to join the community (21–22).

Jonah House, as I mentioned above, is a community that lives together in order to pursue their common Judeo-Christian values. Naar-Obed writes that

> the Sermon on the Mount seems to be most clear about what it means to be Christian. We are told not only to love our neighbor, but our enemy as well. We are told vengeance is no longer acceptable. No more eye for eye and no longer do we fight violence with violence. These instructions make it difficult to remain silent while living in the most militarized nation in the world. (22–23)

The Jonah House community lives together in such a way as to allow the members to speak out against U.S. militarism. They support one another when members participate in nonviolent direct action, whether it is through a demonstration condoned by public officials or an action intended to disarm a nuclear submarine, a felony. The community supports itself by raising much of its food and earns money by painting houses. They live in such a way that if one or several members are gone for an action or to serve a prison sentence as a result of an action, the other members can fill the roles of those who are absent. All of the actions are planned in advance by the community through prayer and discussion.

After joining Jonah House, Naar-Obed met and fell in love with Greg Boertje who was a longtime member of the community. Naar-Obed writes that, "We felt that our union should serve to strengthen each other in our commitment as peacemakers. Our vows to live in voluntary simplicity and to support and love each other during periods of absence due to incarceration for acts of nonviolent resistance were incorporated into our marriage vows" (26). For Naar-Obed and Boertje, marriage deepened their commitment to the Jonah House community and to the world community. From the beginning of their marriage, Naar-Obed and Boertje challenged the view that romantic love inaugurates an isolated, nuclear family. Instead, marriage was integrated into their previous commitment to community engagement.

Naar-Obed and Boertje's marriage demonstrates the kind of relationship that Irigaray recommends in order to welcome a child. Each partner is equal to the other; each gives to the other, and each returns to the self. The relationship between the couple can create the conditions of welcome for a child, who is desired by the couple, but is not necessary to legitimate their relationship. Irigaray describes the path from the horizontal relationship between lovers that can lead them to welcome a child in *Between East and West*:

> Such a loving journey will also lead the man and the woman
> to acquire a possible parental identity. The horizontal coex-
> istence between the sexes, the most necessary coexistence
> between the sexes, the most necessary coexistence, the most
> desirable but also the most difficult to realize, leads naturally
> and spiritually to the respect of ancestors and to hospitality
> toward future generations. (2002, 119)

The relationship between the sexes should not be predicated on the production of a child. A physical relationship between the sexes should focus on the coexistence between two people. The couple's horizontal relationship maintains the difference between the two. They are distinct, respected, and nurtured, but the hierarchy of their difference disappears.

Only after their coexistence becomes fully horizontal can there be a *possibility* of a parental identity.

Maternity

The relationship between a mother and her child—a vertical relationship—ought to be founded on horizontal relationships. When Naar-Obed describes their decision to have a child, the relationships between herself, Boertje, and Jonah House are all central, "We began talking with each other and with our community about our desire for a child with each other and with our community" (27). The decision to have a child clearly came out of a process in which Naar-Obed and Boertje together had a desire for a child. She uses "we" and "our" throughout the description to indicate that she and Boertje together wanted a child. Their decision was also part of the relationship that they shared with others in the community. Just as their marriage was one in which they provided support for each other in order to participate in their community and in society, their decision to have a child was part of their commitment to the world beyond their relationship.

Whereas Baraitser emphasizes the difficulties of the mother-child relationship in Western society, Naar-Obed's narrative offers a scenario in which those difficulties are a result of the sociopolitical context rather than necessarily part of the mother-child relationship. In order to better understand the significance of considering the mother-child relationship in a sociopolitical context, I will consider Amber Jacobs' critique of Irigaray. In "The Potential of Theory: Melanie Klein, Luce Irigaray, and the Mother-Daughter Relationship," Jacobs explores Irigaray's analysis of the mother-daughter relationship (175–193). She admires Irigaray's critique of the mother-daughter relationship as pathological in traditional psychoanalytic theory, but she highlights that Irigaray's use of myth to create a new mother-daughter symbolic order falls prey to patriarchy, "Irigaray, too, cannot seem to avoid reacting to and reproducing the projection onto the maternal that she so forcefully wants to undercut by offering up its opposite: the utopian benign mother who can give her daughter protection from the operations of the father's law that otherwise render her derelict" (185). Jacobs's ultimate conclusion is that theorizing the mother-daughter relationship should start with the absence of a law rather than idealizing the relationship or taking pathology as constitutive of the mother-daughter relationship (191).

In her analysis of Irigaray's work on the mother-daughter relationship, Jacobs does a close textual reading of Irigaray's suggestions of putting up beautiful art in public places that depicts the mother-daughter relationship (Jacobs 180–181; Irigaray 2004, 189). Jacobs is critical of Irigaray's persistently positive language in describing the mother-daughter relationship because that over-idealization misses much of the tension and difficulty in the relationship. I am particularly interested in the final line from the quote that Jacobs uses:

> It [posters in public places showing beautiful images of that natural and spiritual couple, the mother-daughter, the couple that testifies to a very special relationship to nature and culture] will help women move out of the private into the public sphere, out of the family and into the society where they live. (Irigaray 2004, 189)

Jacobs's critique of Irigaray is correct in that idealized images of mothers and daughters are not enough to change a culture that undervalues them. What Jacobs misses, though, is that the traditionally private relationship between mothers and daughters ought to be made public in positive ways that support their relationship. This quote provides a trajectory that allows us to see how Naar-Obed's relationship with her daughter—a vertical relationship founded in her horizontal relationships with her partner and her community—achieves Irigaray's goal of bringing the mother and daughter into society. Naar-Obed brings her relationship into the public by sharing parenting with her partner and her community when she protests U.S. nuclear policy. Naar-Obed also effectively avoids Jacobs's well-formulated critique of Irigaray's idealization of the mother-daughter relationship because she lives a life that supports her mothering and the well-being of her daughter. Naar-Obed's life is a much more concrete step to assure the well-being of mothers and daughters than Irigaray's vague suggestion that beautiful public images will allow the mother-daughter couple to move from the private into the public.

First, we can explore what Irigaray means when she writes that the mother-daughter couple has a "very special relationship to nature and culture." In "How to Ensure the Connection between Natural and Civil Coexistence," Irigaray writes: "The natural survival of the human species has, for centuries, been entrusted above all, to the family: it produces or reproduces life, shelters it, maintains it" (225). In Irigaray's work, "the natural" refers to life, the production of life, and the safe-guarding of life.

She also emphasizes that for humans, the natural always happens in a sociopolitical context. The current sociopolitical context is pathological; it tends to reduce women and children to their roles in the family rather than seeing the family as a place of return out of which each member goes out to the public. The natural is in relationship to the civil. Irigaray further explains what she means by the natural within the context of the family: "This social unit [the family] also represents the place of the return to the state of nature, not only through reproduction and the raising of children but also through bodily and carnal relationships, emotional life, physical rest and regeneration" (225). Irigaray offers a complex understanding of the natural as it functions within a family. The natural can entail having children and raising children, but that happens within a context of physical relationships between other members of the family, especially the physical relationship between parents. The natural also includes our emotions and resting.

This description of the natural understands that the family's ability to carry out their natural tasks is largely dependent on how the natural coexists with the civil. Relationships in which mothers are cut off from the civil and reduced to the natural tasks of mothering can lead to a profound sense of loss when a woman becomes a mother, as Baraitser describes. Irigaray describes another possibility in which the natural and the civil coexist and people can find happiness. For Irigaray, this happens when we find ourselves in nature and in relationships with others (232). The process of finding ourselves in nature and in relationships happens through cultivation of the natural. The idea that humans should culti-vate the natural is precisely what Irigaray means by civil society. Civil society should be founded upon human flourishing instead of economic development.

In *Between East and West*, Irigary describes the family as, "a culti-vation of the union between man and woman in the respect for their differences, which implies that nature becomes consciousness" (118). Cultivation begins in that which is already present: difference, bodies, and nature. Those aspects of the person and the world are brought to our attention and nurtured to produce happiness. Irigaray's discussions of cultivation frequently refer back to her yoga practice, which can deepen our understanding of what she means by cultivation (56–57). Irigaray describes two primary aspects of her yoga practice: breathing and the relationship between student and teacher. For Irigaray, breath indicates autonomy. At birth, breath is our first autonomous gesture (73). Throughout life, cultivating respiration is an opportunity to will autonomy (74). The autonomy that Irigaray emphasizes is balanced by the interdependence of the yoga student and yoga teacher. The relationship between student and teacher indicates the importance of relationship. This relationship transmits "a knowledge useful for a cultivation of life" (58).

The mother who wants to nourish the possibility of happiness in her relationship between herself and her child will have to begin by cultivating her own happiness. She can only hope to have a flourishing relationship with a partner if she is secure in her own difference. She is not reducible to, nor subservient to, her partner. The woman who is autonomous can have a fully horizontal relationship with another that in turn opens the possibility of becoming a mother who will help her child cultivate her/his own life. Yet in Naar-Obed's case, all of these steps transpire in a sociopolitical context that works against the cultivation of life. Within the U.S. context, a mother must come to terms with a culture of death manifested through environmental destruction and military aggression.

Naar-Obed succeeds well in discovering her own purpose, finding a community that will nourish her purpose and be nourished by her, developing a horizontal relationship with her partner, and choosing to become a mother as a further opening of her other relationships rather than a closing of possibility. Yet, she becomes a mother in the United States where money that could be spent on human flourishing (housing, health care, education, child care, art) is diverted to environmentally destructive businesses, weapons, and prisons. When Naar-Obed becomes a mother, she is well aware of the tension between her values and the country's values, and she is committed to a path that challenges the U.S.'s culture of death. During her pregnancy, she becomes increasingly aware of the connection between her own mother-daughter relationship and other mother-child relationships:

> Sometime during my pregnancy, I received a set of pictures of the Hiroshima-Nagasaki bombing. Mostly, they were pictures of the children. One in particular, a burnt and bloodied infant nursing at its mother's burnt and bloody breast, haunted me. After Rachel was born, and especially while I was nursing her, I would visualize that infant in my arms. For a moment, I would become that mother, and the pain I felt was excruciating. More and more, I was drawn to participate in the plowshare witness. I could not let their deaths be in vain.

I would do it for them, for the children that are currently
under threat, and for Rachel [her daughter]. (29)

When she became a mother, Naar-Obed opened to a new empathy
for other mothers, their children, and their suffering. In particular, she
became aware that their suffering could be avoided and was largely
caused by her own country. Her maternity inspired her to participate
in the plowshare witness, nonviolent civil disobedience. The plowshare
witness, though, involves acts meant to reveal the destructive power
of nuclear weapons and citizens' ability to refuse complicity with those
weapons. The witness involves trespassing on property where these weapons are created or stored; it involves symbolically or actually destroying
the weapon, and it involves a symbolic representation of the death that
the weapons cause (generally, witnesses use their own blood poured on
the weapons or on blueprints). Within the United States, these acts are
felony offenses, and witnesses accept imprisonment as a consequence of
their acts. To fulfill her witness, Naar-Obed would almost certainly have
to leave her daughter, who inspired her to act (15).

Social Transformation

The most challenging critique to consider when we think about mothers who intentionally commit felony acts as a form of social protest is
whether a symbolic act can justify concrete sacrifice. The felony act is
unlikely to create any change in social policy and very limited change
in public opinion, but the relationship with their children is very likely
to be harmed. Naar-Obed's action, though, disrupts the calculus that
most of us would use to determine whether or not to act.

While most of us cannot understand why anyone would risk a long
prison sentence for something that is unlikely to produce the change that
one desires, Daniel Berrigan offers an important model of the motivation
that inspires many activists. In the film, The Catonsville Nine: Investigation of a Flame, Berrigan describes the process of deciding to participate
in burning draft files with homemade napalm, and he says that he could
not, not participate (Sachs). Normally, this sort of double negative would
make no sense to a listener, but in this case, it describes the way in
which Berrigan chose to do something that he did not want to do. His
response emphasizes his reluctance and his commitment to the act; he

had to participate. Many of our actions are determined by what we want to do: we want to go for a walk on a nice day, we want to eat our favorite foods, we want to spend time with our friends. Other actions are determined by what we want to get from the action: we want to lose weight by going for a walk or giving up our favorite foods, we want knee replacement surgery in order to walk without pain. Berrigan, however, knew that burning draft files would not end the Vietnam War, and he knew that he would go to prison for being part of the act. Nevertheless, Berrigan chose to be part of the protest and to accept consequences that would not be pleasurable.

Berrigan certainly was not physically forced to participate in this act, which means we have to seek another explanation for why he "could not" not participate. Many years after the action I have described above, I heard Berrigan give a public lecture and answer questions at Fordham University. One student asked Berrigan why he participates in these kinds of protests when he does not expect them to produce changes in policy. Berrigan responded that he did not engage in that sort of cost-benefit analysis. Instead, he decides whether or not the act is the right thing to do. If it is right, he acts. For him, an act is right when it upholds the dignity of the person, is nonviolent, and announces a new possibility. He decided to burn the draft files because it was the right thing to do regardless of the results or consequences.

Naar-Obed and Berrigan have similar motives for their actions. Both look at the militarism in U.S. society and feel compelled to act. Berrigan participated in burning the draft files of hundreds of men during the Vietnam War by using homemade napalm. His act is very clear in its purpose and meaning: the Vietnam War was wrong and the United States ought not to use napalm bombs against people; the U.S. government was wrong to draft men to participate in this unethical war and burning the draft files will impede the government's ability to do so. Naar-Obed's ethical message is also clear: the U.S. government is wrong to stockpile nuclear weapons. Both affirm the dignity of every person by destroying—physically, for Berrigan, symbolically, for Naar-Obed—things that would destroy people. Both use nonviolent methods; they do not injure people nor any property that sustains people. While some would argue that they destroy property—draft files, for example—Berrigan and Naar-Obed argue that only things that are "proper" to human beings' flourishing are property. Nuclear weapons and draft files are part of a culture of death and not property according to this perspective. The final motive for their acts is to announce a new possibility. Both announce the possibility of international relations built on cooperation rather than force and violence.

Berrigan's use of napalm to destroy the draft files may strike some as violent even if they grant that the draft files themselves are the means of perpetrating an injustice against U.S. citizens and Vietnam citizens. For Berrigan and Naar-Obed, though, the use of napalm to destroy draft files is not a violent act since the act is a means to destroy that which would cause real harm. Napalm is the appropriate choice in this instance because it opens people's eyes to the effects of napalm so they can understand what is happening to *people* in Vietnam. The act of destroying the files also announces that people have a choice to refuse complicity in the violence and harm happening in Vietnam.

While the comparison between Berrigan and Naar-Obed is useful to understand why they act, this comparison becomes strained when we consider that Berrigan is a Jesuit priest and Naar-Obed is a mother. When Berrigan chose to participate in a nonviolent protest that would lead to a felony conviction, he had to consider the cost of this action to himself and to his order. While his sentence would put a strain on the community, others in the community could compensate for Berrigan's absence. He also knew that serving time in a federal prison would be an incredibly unpleasant experience, but he was willing to choose that suffering for the sake of those in Vietnam who had no choice about being there.

Naar-Obed had to consider her community, her husband, and her young daughter. The concerns that we might have about the effects of Naar-Obed's actions on her community and her husband are relatively easy to dispense with since both encouraged her and fully supported her decision to symbolically disarm a nuclear submarine. Her daughter, however, was much too young to appreciate what her mother was doing, what the effects would be, and to consent. All of these considerations are true for any parent of a 23-month-old child. At 23 months, my son, Asher, would bite people. When he did this, he would get a time out. He had no idea why biting resulted in a time out, and he certainly did not consent to a time out. From his perspective, biting worked: he bit another child and the child gave him the toy he wanted. The perspective I wanted him to learn was that we don't bite, not even if someone has done something mean to us, and not even if it gets us what we want. At 23 months, I was trying to instill values that he would hopefully understand later. Naar-Obed's separation from her daughter was also intended to instill values and provide an example that her daughter would understand later.

Naar-Obed knew her daughter would be well loved and well cared for in her absence. She also knew her absence would be less disruptive for her daughter than it would be in a nuclear family. Her daughter had always been parented by many of the adults in the community, not just her mother and her father. Naar-Obed had the opportunity to model alternatives to the value placed on violence in U.S. society. Her act would not actually disarm a nuclear submarine, but it would state that the violence and destruction built into this weapon is wrong and that U.S. citizens do not have to be passive when we see that something is wrong regardless of whether or not this particular act will produce the change that we desire. She introduced her daughter to the idea that a person can act based on an analysis of right and wrong instead of calculating costs against benefits.

In response to a question about her decision to act while her daughter was so young, Naar-Obed responds: "When is the right time? Do I do it now when she's a toddler? Do I wait till she's 5 in grade school, in high school? There is never a good time/Whenever I choose to do this, I will always miss a part of her life and I always think about the women who had no choice" (Gross 6). Ultimately, Naar-Obed's act is not that different from the decisions that mothers make every day. We set up the conditions we believe will make our children's flourishing possible. We fight against conditions that interfere with their flourishing. We hope the sacrifices we make and discipline we enforce while our children are too young to understand will make sense to our children as they grow. We hope that our children will choose to pursue what is right even when others give up, when it is difficult, and when they may not be compensated for doing the right thing.

Naar-Obed's choice to participate in a Plowshares' witness might be criticized by those who believe that she neglected the care of her daughter. This criticism, though, mistakenly assumes that mothering is an activity that only happens in the relationship between a mother and a child. Naar-Obed's mother-child relationship is intersubjective; it arises from her commitment to her partner and to her community. Naar-Obed writes, "Rachel thrived during my absence. She was given much love, and she in turn enriched the lives of those around her" (23). Certainly, Naar-Obed missed her daughter and missed the daily, corporeal tasks of mothering, but those tasks were entrusted to the community and the partner with whom she chose to have a child. Naar-Obed's act also allowed her to cultivate an awareness of the connection between all people and her daughter. She gives us an example in which maternity is joyful, hopeful, and a continuation of the mother's projects. Further, she offers an example of the mother-child relationship that does not depend on an impossible idealization of the world. Instead, she faces that which is destructive in U.S. culture and uses her opposition to that culture to cultivate new ways of living with her child, her partner, her community, and her society.

Naar-Obed's example of mothering that provides inspiration for new ways of living in community, marriage, and a world without war helps to challenge the idea that U.S. militarism, isolated mothering, and patriarchal models of marriage are the only possible ways to live. While her story is one rooted in hope and possibility, we should also consider the ways in which grief can bring out awareness of the harms of militarism and the pressing need for immediate change. Cindy Sheehan's biography of maternal activism is born out of her grief and despair when her son Casey dies rather than the hopefulness for a different future that gives birth to Naar-Obed's activism.

4

Cindy Sheehan

War and Institutionalized Misinformation

Molly Rush's and Michele Naar-Obed's protests focused on the increasing possibility of a nuclear exchange between the U.S. and the former USSR: these mothers focused on bringing attention to the nuclear buildup in the United States; on exposing the ways in which producing nuclear weapons makes all humans vulnerable; and on debunking the myth that building up the military and weapons stockpile protects us. While both Rush and Naar-Obed fear what would happen to their children and children around the world if these weapons are used, Cindy Sheehan's protests and activism happen because she has had to endure the nightmare of losing her son in war. Sheehan's protest focuses on the very concrete reality of the harm that comes from war. The harms that they bring to light are actual; they are realized possibilities. As with Rush and Naar-Obed, Sheehan successfully resists U.S. society's pressure to stay silent. Although their actions may jeopardize the privileges that they enjoy as white, American women, they reject mainstream approval in order to speak out, act, and make actual and potential suffering visible. They focus attention on the possibility of withdrawing consent and acting nonviolently against a seemingly impenetrable system. Their actions reveal that anyone can act, and in turn their actions reveal that silence in the face of injustice is complicity.

When Casey Sheehan died, his mother began to question U.S. militarism and why U.S. leaders use the military to settle abstract political disputes. Through her protests, others have had the opportunity to question the idea that the very concrete reality of killing and dying produces abstract goods such as freedom and democracy in other countries. Most of the time, white, middle-class people can sit back and declare that something must be done about terrorism without thinking about

65

the people who are killing and being killed in order to supposedly do something. Sheehan's grief for her son takes away the luxury of ignoring the concrete realities of militarism. The abstract idea of dying for one's country is replaced by the concrete reality of a woman mourning her son.

In the summer of 2005, Cindy Sheehan began trying to meet with President George W. Bush to ask him why the United States is waging a war in Iraq, a war that caused the death of her son, Casey. Because Bush resolutely refused to meet with Sheehan, she engaged in protesting outside of his ranch in Texas, followed him as he travelled around the country, and staged a hunger strike in Washington DC. For months, the media was captivated by Sheehan's persistence. Some observers were moved by the plight of a mother searching for meaning in her son's death. Other observers seemed to be outraged by a mother who would demand accountability from the President of the United States. Central to many of the responses are certain beliefs about what mothers ought to do when moved to act politically as mothers.

Sheehan's quest to ask questions about, and find meaning in, her son's death reflects many of the virtues of maternal work that are recognized by American society and highlighted in Sara Ruddick's book, *Maternal Thinking: Toward a Politics of Peace* (1995) that I focused on in Chapter 2. In her persistent questioning and protests, Sheehan reveals the ambiguity inherent in mothering in the United States. First, if a mother says nothing and does nothing about the pervasive militarism in society, the very lives of her children (as well as other children) are at risk. Yet, if a mother speaks out against militarism or commits an act of civil disobedience, she risks scorn and imprisonment that can interfere with, or make impossible, much of the work of mothering. Second, part of mothering involves raising children to be socially acceptable, but in a militaristic society that which is socially acceptable is morally unacceptable. Sheehan would come to realize that by unreflectively supporting institutions that support militarism and becoming distracted by entertainment rather than being informed about her government, she played a role in her son's death. She, then, uses the knowledge of how she unknowingly supported militarism to speak out against it and to provide others an opportunity to live more conscientiously.

The Cold War and the War on Terror

While it may seem unusual to compare Rush's and Naar-Obed's actions against the nuclear buildup during the Cold War to Sheehan's actions in 2005, and the Cold War to the "War on Terror," the commonalities in their struggles illustrate the on-going militarism that pacifist mothers are actively trying to oppose and their ambiguous situation wrought by a conflict between what is socially valued and what is morally imperative (Woehrle, Coy and Maney 144). In both cases, most Americans kept silent about U.S. militarism out of fear. During the Cold War, people lived in fear of a nuclear exchange between the United States and the then-USSR. Americans believed that having more and bigger weapons than the Soviets would keep nuclear exchange from happening. During the Iraq and Afghanistan wars, U.S. citizens live in fear that if we are not fighting in Afghanistan and Iraq, then terrorists will attack the United States. In *Contesting Patriotism: Culture, Power, and Strategy in the Peace Movement,* Lynne M. Woehrle, Patrick G. Coy, and Gregory M. Maney research the dominant media stories about threats from Iraq during the period beginning September 11, 2001 and continuing through approximately 2005 (83–92). Their research reveals the ways in which the Bush administration stoked the fears of the U.S. population to garner support for the Iraq War. These fears caused most Americans to avert their gaze from the realities of their eras: the threat of nuclear weapons during the Cold War and the reality of violence in the War against Terror. These mothers courageously spoke out and focused public attention on the reality of militarism.

The connection between the Cold War and the War against Terror also has to do with the way in which an enemy is produced in order to unite Americans in a common fear. In *Abolition Democracy*, Angela Y. Davis explains this connection: ". . . I would like to suggest that the terrain for the production of the terrorist as a figure in the American imaginary reflects vestiges of previous moral panics as well, including those instigated by the mass fear of the criminal and the communist" (45). Davis emphasizes that Americans' fears about terrorists, criminals, and communists stem from imagined dangers rather than from actual knowledge. The effect of the unifying fear is that Americans create an enemy both inside and outside the nation (46). The external enemy justifies military force and military buildup to protect the United States. During the Cold War, the United States built up nuclear weapons to protect its citizens from the Soviets and their presumed military power. During the War against Terror, the United States justifies military engagement and occupation, torture, mass imprisonment abroad, and reduced civil liberties at home by claiming to protect U.S. citizens from terrorists. Because of her experience as a mother, Sheehan has an empathy for other mothers and for children that allows her to confront U.S. militarism and to reveal that much of what U.S. society fears is an illusion.

Against the Iraq War

In memoirs, newspaper interviews, or biographies, each of the mothers in this book describes something that happens in their lives, which changes their perspective, so they can no longer remain silent about the injustice they see around them. Cindy Sheehan's moment of change is an experience so heart-wrenching and so filled with pain that the narrative can be difficult to read at times; her moment of radicalization comes when her son, Casey, is killed in Iraq. The suffering she endures when she learns that Casey was killed in combat is what I would describe as an "aha" moment, or a moment when something hidden is revealed with such clarity that it is impossible to see the world in any other way forever after that moment. At first, she simply knows that Casey's death is not right, but in her struggle to understand that wrong she sheds light on the wrongness of the Iraq War and war itself.

Throughout her speeches, letters, and writing, Sheehan begins her story with descriptions of Casey's life. She describes her joy of becoming a mother, the kind, sweet nature of her son, and the strength of the bond between them. She continually emphasizes how close their relationship was, doing everything from participating in the youth ministry at their church (Sheehan was the youth minister) to frequently going to movies together (2006a, 63; 2006b, 32). When we consider how much her life revolved around Casey and her other children and that her very definition of herself was "mother of four," we can certainly understand how devastating the news of her son's death was and why it transformed her (2006b, 242).

In describing the wrongness of her son's death Sheehan uses the term "disordered" (2006b, 23, 84). Her first reference to Casey's death as disordered is a literal reference to birth order and death order, and she describes the difference between burying her father and burying her son. While the death of a parent is painful and the loss is significant, a mother expects to outlive her parents and their deaths are part of a comprehensible (albeit difficult) order. When her child dies, though, the expected order of death is turned upside down and throws Sheehan's world into question.

In the first weeks after Casey's death, even her capacity to mother her surviving children was destroyed: "As I have stated before, I was a horrible mother to my other three children after Casey was killed. It seemed that they had to spend all of their time comforting me. I was in such a dark place of pain and regret that I could not even begin to be a mother to them" (2006b, 124). The disorder in Sheehan's life reshapes everything in the weeks following her son's death: she's a mother who must bury her son, and her children must comfort her. This disordered state leads to Sheehan awakening to a new purpose in her life that begins as her daughter, Carly, confronts her mother's despair in a poem she writes and then reads to her mother, "Have you ever heard the sounds of a mother screaming for her son? / The torrential weeping of a mother will never be done, / They call him a hero, you should be glad he's one, but, / have you ever heard the sounds of a mother weeping for her son?" (2005, 195). It is this very poem that helped Sheehan translate this overwhelming grief into activism, "Have you ever heard the sound of a nation being rocked to sleep? / The leaders want to keep you numb so the pain won't be so deep. / But if we the people let them continue, another mother will weep. / Have you ever heard the sounds of a nation being rocked to sleep?" (Sheehan 194). Sheehan's quest for justice for her son, for other mothers, and for their children begins not only as a result of the devastating death of her son and the circumstances surrounding his death, but also in the clarity of the message from her daughter, which allowed Sheehan to focus her energy on keeping the nation from being rocked to sleep. Hearing this poem is the "aha" moment that begins Sheehan's activism.

The focus of her activism, especially in its earliest days, centers on the extreme pain of losing her oldest son, Casey to an unjust war that never should have happened. When Sheehan writes essays, gives speeches, and sends letters, she consistently speaks out against then-President George W. Bush and then-Defense Secretary Donald Rumsfeld; in particular, she criticizes their decision to go to war in Iraq. She focuses much of her attention on the ways in which the U.S. public and soldiers were misled and lied to about the need for a war in Iraq, citing as evidence the fact that the 9/11 commission found no link between the September 11, 2001 terrorism and Iraq, no link between Al-Qaeda and Saddam Hussein, and no link between Osama Bin Laden and Saddam Hussein. In each of her books, Sheehan also points to the proof she discovered that Iraq never had Weapons of Mass Destruction and that supposed evidence of WMDs was misleading or manufactured. David Kay, the lead weapons inspector in Iraq, has indeed revealed that there is no evidence that Iraq does now, or did prior to the March 2003 invasion, possess weapons of mass destruction. But, even before the war began many people knew that Saddam Hussein could not have weapons of mass destruction.

While Sheehan does not discover the extent of misinformation used by the Bush administration to invade Iraq until after Casey's death, her discoveries point to information available before the war that should have stopped the administration from invading Iraq. In the days leading up to the invasion, Colin Powell presented the United States' case for invasion to the United Nations Security Council. However, all of his information (including photos, taped conversations, and film footage) was subject to criticism even before the United States began its war. Prior to the war, Maria Tomchick, an American journalist, wrote "Powell's Flimsy Evidence" in which she raised a series of questions about Powell's evidence of weapons of mass destruction in Iraq, which came from undocumented sources, contained blurred images, and showed empty trucks (Tomchick). Her conclusion, long before Kay's report and in time to prevent the war, is that at best the evidence is too murky to justify an invasion; at worst, she believes the evidence may be fabricated.

As Arundhati Roy observed in her criticisms of the U.S. (and allies') invasion of Iraq, "In the fog of war—one thing's for sure—if Saddam's regime indeed has weapons of mass destruction, it is showing an astonishing degree of responsibility and restraint in the teeth of extreme provocation" (34–35). Her comments were made after the war began, but the same reasoning applied even before the "shock and awe" campaign, and Sheehan makes this same argument against the war in Iraq. Either Saddam Hussein had WMDs or he didn't. If he had none, then he wasn't a imminent threat to the United States. If he had WMDs, and he chose not to use them, then he still wasn't a threat. If he wasn't a threat, then the United States had no justification for its preemptive strike against Iraq.

In addition to the lies that led to the invasion of Iraq, Sheehan recounts in many places the lies that led young people, particularly Casey, to enlist in the Army. Casey was promised a $20,000 enlistment bonus and only received $4,500, he was promised that he could finish his college degree but no classes were ever approved, he was told that he would be a chaplain's assistant (he was a Humvee mechanic), and most importantly for his mother, that he would never see combat, but he died in a combat rescue mission (2005, 8).

As Sheehan reflects on the lies that led Casey to join the Army (which in turn would place Casey in harm's way when Bush declared war on Iraq), we are led to reflect on what it means to say that Casey joined the Army voluntarily and voluntarily went on the combat mission in which he was killed. The very idea that his act could be voluntary is thrown into question if he did not have access to information about the choice he was making, or if he was deliberately given false information. Throughout her work, Sheehan stresses the seeming contradiction between Casey enlisting in the Army and the boy he was, one who was kind and gentle and so religious that people expected him to become a priest. In part his decision can be explained by the lies his recruiter told him in order to convince Casey to enlist in the first place. While others expected Casey to become a priest, he wanted to get married and have children and to complete his college degree; nevertheless, he did want to care for people and live out his Catholic faith. The recruiter, according to his mother, played on all of these hopes for his future, promising college tuition and a job as a chaplain's assistant. Moreover, when Casey enlisted, the country was not at war and George W. Bush was not yet president. From this perspective and the assurance of the recruiter, neither Casey nor his family expected him to be part of any combat.

Certainly, the lies that Sheehan describes the military recruiter telling her son cannot be substantiated definitively, but the testimony of other recruits and undercover investigations of recruiting practices all make it highly probable that Casey was, at the very least, misled as to the likelihood of his being an assistant chaplain, the signing bonus he would receive, the ease with which he would be able to complete his degree, and the impossibility of ever seeing combat (Dakss; White). Yet, Sheehan also recounts that people have argued that Casey chose to reenlist and chose to go on a combat mission to rescue other soldiers. Thus, even if we grant that his original choice to enlist was coerced, we must still consider whether his later choices—when he already knew the original promises to be false—were made freely.

Sheehan gives two responses to the idea that Casey's reenlistment and volunteering for combat were free choices. First, she points to Casey's character and his concern for others: "Casey didn't agree with the 'Mission' [the war in Iraq], but being the courageous and honorable man that he was, he knew he had to go to this mistake of a war to support his buddies" (2005, 14). In another chapter, Sheehan writes, "Yes, Casey did enlist and re-enlist in the Army. He loved being a soldier, and he loved his buddies. He was a good soldier, and he volunteered for the dangerous mission he was killed on" (2005, 12). In addition to taking advantage of his character to get him to reenlist, his concern for others is something that could have been exploited for the rescue mission, hence: "The first chance he got, my brave, wonderful faithful, sweet, gentle, and kind boy volunteered for a rescue mission as a Combat Life Saver" (2005, 9).

Sheehan's second reason for calling into question how free Casey was to reenlist and to take part in the rescue mission is that she hears over and over again that soldiers are pressured and lied to in order to get them to reenlist. Sheehan listens to both the experiences of other parents whose children enlisted and the veterans themselves, and their experiences tell a consistent story of deception during recruitment and pressure to reenlist or face "stop-loss" in which soldiers would be forced to continue their service, but without the compensation that they supposedly would receive by reenlisting (2005, 28–31). Accounts of war from other soldiers also lead Sheehan to question whether Casey freely volunteered for the rescue mission. Sheehan writes: "Other soldiers from Vietnam and Iraq tell me that this is the way 99 percent of soldiers volunteer: The superior points at each soldier and says, 'You, you, you, and you: you volunteer'" (2006, 51). Although Sheehan talks to as many people involved in the combat mission as she can and reads as much material as she can, the answers to what happened that day remains a mystery. Nevertheless, Sheehan reaches one conclusion: the Iraq War was a mistake orchestrated by George W. Bush. This conclusion leads her to work toward ending the war and to demand that Bush account for his actions.

The intensity of Sheehan's grief, the clarity of her demand for accountability from the president, and her tireless work to expose the truth that the war in Iraq was unnecessary and avoidable all came together to capture the attention of the United States. For many people, Sheehan's message echoed their own grief and disgust with the war. Others wanted her to be silent and not raise questions that had no answer, or at least not an answer that those in power wanted to make public. For those on both sides of the issue, Sheehan's status as the mother of a soldier killed in combat was central.

In her article, "Grieving Dead Soldiers, Disavowing Loss: Sheehan and the Im/possibility of the American Antiwar Movement," Tina Managhan traces the antiwar rhetoric of the Iraq and Afghanistan wars to show that even those opposed to the war voiced support for the troops, and that voicing support for the troops was a necessary precondition of voiding antiwar sentiments in the popular culture (441–442). She continues her analysis of the antiwar rhetoric by focusing on Sheehan's role as a catalyst for the antiwar movement. Managhan suggests that it was Sheehan who crystallized the notion of supporting the troops by bringing them home, and through this message Sheehan both becomes her "real self" and the icon of the antiwar movement. In her descriptions of Sheehan, Managhan uses the words "real," "authentic," and "legitimate" (442–447.). She chooses these words to describe the way in which Sheehan's message was made possible by increasing antiwar sentiment in the country, respect for troops, and respect for grieving mothers. Managhan does not suggest that Sheehan's grief or demand for answers was insincere, rather she suggests the conditions were ripe in the United States for a spokesperson to come forward and voice people's complicated sentiments about the war.

Against War and For Peace

As Sheehan develops her position and her activism a shift takes place in her message; she moves from critiquing the Iraq War and U.S. leaders (especially, George W. Bush and Donald Rumsfeld) for pushing the United States into the war to a critique of war in general and focusing on a broad critique of U.S. society's culture of militarism in which she unknowingly participated.

The first written evidence of this shift occurs in her essay, "What Kind of Extremist Will You Be?" and links her critiques of war to the critiques that Martin Luther King, Jr. makes in his "Letter from a Birmingham Jail." In response to criticism that he is an extremist, King replies that he is an extremist for love, truth, and justice (298). Sheehan follows King's lead in this essay and links the Cold War to the Iraq War and to war in general, placing herself on the side of extremism for love, truth, and justice (2005, 189–192). Her message of love, truth, and justice becomes a focal point of much of her work after this essay. She is no longer working only to stop the Iraq War; she is working for peace.

Love

A powerful source of the love Sheehan manifests comes from her background in the Roman Catholic Church. Sheehan, like Rush and Naar-Obed, brings to her activism a familiarity with Catholic Social Teaching and through that an understanding of the preciousness of human life, which leads to an obligation to care for those lives. As a believer, she is able to cut through the shallow rhetoric of "protecting life" that politicians use when it is convenient for their cause and overlook when

it becomes inconvenient. While much of the United States (Roman
Catholics included) has come to view the Roman Catholic Church's
teaching on an ethics of life as focused only on abortion issues, Sheehan's
analysis serves to highlight that debates on abortion distract citizens from
larger life, which she brings back into focus.

In March 2005, the media focused its attention on a battle between
members of Terry Schiavo's family on whether or not she should be
allowed to die or be kept alive with intravenous feeding and hydration.
The Florida battle captured attention around the nation with politicians,
Catholic hierarchy, and media all weighing in with their opinions. When
Bush weighs in to support keeping Schiavo alive ("When in Doubt, It Is
Always Better To Err on the Side of Life"—March 22, 2005), Sheehan
berates him for his hypocrisy. "But I do have one question for Congress
and for George Bush, though: Why does Terry Schiavo deserve to live
more than my son, Spc. Casey Austin Sheehan, did?" (2006, 17). She
continues to make her point by writing:

> Instead of a culture of life, this administration has promoted
> the opposite: from Bush's signing into Texas law the Futile Care
> Bill, to the culture of the death penalty in Texas (and around
> our nation), proposed cuts in Medicaid, and laws restricting
> medical malpractice lawsuits and Chapter 7 bankruptcy for
> families who have incurred huge medical bills. (2006, 18)

Sheehan's list of violations against a culture of life promotes the idea
that rather than creating conditions for life to flourish, Bush is creating
a culture of death. The idea of a culture of death should be understood
in the context of Sheehan's Catholic background, and Pope John Paul
II clearly articulates what the culture of death is and why it destroys
life when he says:

> This reality [a veritable structure of sin] is characterized by
> the emergence of a culture which denies solidarity and in
> many cases takes the form of a veritable 'culture of death.'
> This culture is actively fostered by powerful cultural, eco-
> nomic and political currents which encourage an idea of
> society excessively concerned with efficiency. Looking at the
> situation from this point of view, it is possible to speak in
> a certain sense of a war of the powerful against the weak: a

life which would require greater acceptance, love and care is
considered useless, or held to be an intolerable burden, and is
therefore rejected in one way or another . . . This conspiracy
involves not only individuals in their personal, family or group
relationships, but goes far beyond, to the point of damaging
and distorting, at the international level, relations between
peoples and States. (12)

While Bush chooses to use arguments in defense of life selectively, Sheehan's list of cuts to social programs, increased use of the death penalty,
use of war, and economic limits on legal protections for families exposes
that Bush's actions lead toward a culture of death in which not only are
individuals damaged, but global relationships between peoples of different
nations and between states are distorted such that rather than increasing
love and acceptance, the powerful inflict their will on the weak.

Sheehan, in contrast, deliberately works to create a culture of peace
in which she reaches out to others who can support her message against
the Iraq War, but she also reaches out to those who disagree with her.
During her time at Camp Casey, she titles her reflection on Day Eight,
as "Hope is Blossoming;" in this section she describes the way in which
the huge community of people who have supported her and her cause
has gained the attention of the mainstream media and caused people
to question Bush, Rumsfeld, and the war in Iraq. She also describes the
way in which this movement has served to demonstrate that one person
can make a difference. "Before Casey was killed, I didn't think that one
person could ever make a difference in the world. Now I know that
isn't true. Not only can one person make a difference, but one person,
with millions behind her, can make history . . . hope is blossoming in
Crawford, Texas, because *we* have power" (2005, 92). The power that
Sheehan discovers is that when injustice is happening many people know
that it is wrong and want to do something, but they do nothing because
they think that one person cannot make a difference; however, when
someone steps forward, that can be enough to get those who thought
they were alone to become active. In this same post, Sheehan describes
her meeting with a father whose son was also killed in Iraq and who
believes that the Iraq War is a noble cause. Clearly, the two have divergent views on the war, but Sheehan listens to him and befriends him.
"By the end of the day, we were drinking beer together and telling each
other, 'I love you'" (2005, 93–94).

Truth

While love is a central part of Sheehan's message, she also has a clear commitment to making sure that the truth about the Iraq War and war in general is told. As part of this commitment to telling the truth, Sheehan spends much of her time speaking to people in the media, but her relationship to the media is ambivalent since the mainstream media is both the key to reaching the average U.S. citizen and frequently a tool of the powerful to distract people from truth.

To begin to understand the ways in which popular media has distracted people from understanding the effects of war, we can use an analysis similar to the one in which Sheehan engages throughout her work. She begins to analyze the lead up to the Iraq War by focusing on September 11, 2001. She emphasizes throughout her work that the Bush administration continuously linked 9/11 to Saddam Hussein even after the 9/11 Commission submitted its final report definitively stating that there was no connection between the September 11 attacks and Saddam Hussein. Nevertheless, the events of 9/11 opened what Žižek calls the "desert of the real," a phrase that he takes from the movie, *The Matrix* (Wachowski):

> The material reality we all experience and see around us is a virtual one, generated and coordinated by a gigantic megacomputer to which we are all attached; when the hero (played by Keanu Reeves) awakens in the "real reality," he sees a desolate landscape littered with burned ruins—what remained of Chicago after a global war. The resistance leader Morpheus utters the ironic greeting: "Welcome to the desert of the real." (386)

"The desert of the real" is the reality behind the virtual reality, a field of desolation hidden by a shiny veneer of prosperity and safety. The desert of the real is a frightening place and exposes people to their vulnerability, which is not only uncomfortable, but was unfamiliar in the United States. Throughout the Cold War, U.S. citizens believed that the military and weapons in this country and among our allies would protect them. The collapse of the Soviet Union seemed to confirm the illusion of invincibility. While the revelation that we are all vulnerable could have been the result of the terrible attacks of 9/11, the Bush administration, with the cooperation of the media, worked to reestablish the illusion of absolute power by first staging a military attack against Afghanistan and then staging the Iraq War.

Sheehan points out that Bush played on people's fears and linked 9/11 to Saddam Hussein in speech after speech and also stoked people's fears by stating that Iraq had weapons of mass destruction, contrary to the reports that were subsequently released (2005, 23). Although many journalists and academics were questioning the need for a war in Iraq, in the lead-up to the war Bush linked Hussein and Al-Qaeda so successfully that polls by *New York Times*/CBS News, and ABC News indicated that between 42 and 55 percent of U.S. citizens believed that Saddam Hussein was directly responsible for the 9/11 attacks (Roy 43).

Just as disturbing as the Bush administration's rush to war and misrepresentation of the facts is that the media was complicit in encouraging excitement for the war instead of encouraging critical discussion and asking probing questions about why the United States was going into a war unilaterally. Consider, for example, the soundtracks used by the various media outlets as they covered "the shock and awe" phase of the 2003 Iraq War; each of the cable news channels developed music that heightened the feeling of crisis (Engstrom 46). According to Nicholas Engstrom, the preparations for these soundtracks began well in advance of the actual breakout of war:

> Five days before the war with Iraq began, I visited Fox News headquarters to pick up a CK labeled "Liberation Iraq Music," containing what was to be the theme music for the war coverage. The Fox theme could be Metallica rehearsing Wagner, the guitar chords rising over thudding drums. It seemed readymade for *Apocalypse Now*, when helicopters blare *The Flight of the Valkyries* from mounted speakers as they swoop down on a Vietcong-held village. Would the coverage fit the music? (45)

The fact that Engstrom compares Fox News Channel's (FNC) war music to movie scenes emphasizes the way in which even supposedly objective sources of news are giving viewers a narrow perspective on what was happening in Iraq. We could imagine a quite different soundtrack in which heart-wrenching music is used to emphasize the suffering and plight of Iraqi citizens whose infrastructure and lives are falling to ruins as the United States stages its "shock and awe" campaign. We can easily imagine that Sheehan would have chosen very different music to convey her fears for her son who was in the military and faced the possibility of being sent to war in Iraq. However, CNN, FNC, MSNBC, and CBS all relied on music that heightened identification with the American military (both its soldiers and its technology) to help deliver and determine the content of their coverage of the initial U.S. invasion of Iraq (Engstrom 46–47).

While the soundtracks used by the major news networks may lead us to suspect that the Iraq War coverage is biased, we must look to the actual content of the news to determine whether or not this is true. For anyone who has watched the news, it will come as no surprise that the coverage of events does vary slightly depending on which cable news network we consider. A study of CNN and FNC, which are perceived by many to be liberal and conservative respectively, reveals that the content of the news is the same on both networks; the distinction between these networks is the manner in which news is delivered. While FNC relies heavily on opinionated journalists to deliver the news, CNN relies on calm staid journalists to deliver the news (Farhi 1–2). Overall, FNC's manner of delivering news results in the most biased coverage (Aday, Livingston and Hebert). In "Embedding the Truth: A Cross-Cultural Analysis of Objectivity and Television Coverage of the Iraq War," Sean Aday, Steven Livingston, and Macye Hebert carried out a comprehensive study of 1,820 news stories on ABC, Al-Jazeera, CBS, CNN, NBC, and FNC in order to determine whether or not these popular media outlets have a bias when they try to deliver objective news (7–9). They examined these networks' objectivity at two levels:

> First, it must look at coverage at the story level. It must examine the objectivity of individual stories and compare the overall body of work at various networks and, in this case, across cultures. Second, such an examination must look at the overall picture of the war offered by the various news organizations. For example, it may be that stories are objective but that a bias can be seen in the relative selection and avoidance of certain story topics. (8)

At the level of the story, all of the networks, except FNC, maintained an overall neutrality. FNC's coverage of the war was deemed biased largely because of its reporters' identification with individual troops and the U.S. military ("our troops") (8–13). The bias of FNC coverage, though, also included one anchor calling antiwar protestors "sickening" (10). The bias of FNC coverage was significant as compared to other networks:

In addition [to bias from interviews with retired military], much of the pro-war slant in stories came in stories where the anchor was the primary reporter (e.g., stories read or interviews conducted by the anchor), with 66.7 percent of these adopting a supportive tone. This compares to a range of 3.3 to 8.5 percent of the anchor-led stories on the other American networks. (14)

The overall conclusions of the authors of this study is that FNC's decision to encourage the use of first-person plural in reporters' coverage of the Iraq War is significant because it encourages a pro-war stance in its viewing audience. The bias that this affects in viewers is all the more significant, according to the authors, because FNC viewers already tend to be pro-administration and pro-war (18).

A clear message that comes out of Sheehan's experiences with the news networks is that U.S. citizens are continually distracted from pressing political issues. For example, when Sheehan was scheduled for an interview on *Larry King Live*, she was bumped from the interview so Larry King could cover the Michael Jackson alleged-molestation trial instead (2005, 14–16). Certainly, child molestation is a serious issue deserving in-depth coverage, but this was coverage of a celebrity much more than it was coverage of the vulnerability of children and the circumstances that lead to that vulnerability. Even when the news networks are not manipulating people's emotions with soundtracks and providing accurate information about the stories that they do cover, they still fail to be objective when they choose to cover speculation about celebrities rather than asking questions or providing multiple views about the Iraq War.

The conclusion in "Embedding the Truth" is that the popular media operates with a bias by virtue of what they cover and what they do not cover. The bias comes from the sanitized version of events (no blood, no casualties even when embedded journalists cover fighting), the lack of coverage of dissent, and the lack of coverage of international diplomatic efforts to prevent and halt the war (3, 16–18). While this study confirms popular opinion and other research that FNC is particularly guilty of constructing a highly edited and artificial version of reality, it also reveals the ways in which the major popular U.S. media outlets are using standards of neutrality to conceal bias at other levels. Very few individual stories are guilty of extreme bias—less than 1 percent according to Aday, Livingston, and Hebert's research (12); nevertheless, the overall coverage of the war is largely supportive and uncritical.

This research is also supported by Jules Boykoff in *Beyond Bullets: The Suppression of Dissent in the U.S.* in which she details the many ways in which the U.S. government has stifled critical media coverage (2007).

Even when Sheehan begins to receive some positive media coverage in the *New York Times, The Washington Post,* and Clear Channel Radio Stations during her vigil outside Bush's Texas ranch (Rich), other popular media outlets continue to disparage her and focus their attention on her problems with her husband. The focus of media attention on the separation and divorce made the focus of this very personal and painful event an opportunity for detractors to draw conclusions about the cause of the divorce (2006, 123–132). Sheehan documents the way in which her detractors try to distract people from her message by focusing attention on her family and the struggles that she has had, especially with her husband. Rather than debating the facts that she discovers, the morality of war in general, or the morality of the Iraq War, in particular, some in the media began to focus on every step of her divorce from her husband of 28 years (2005, 99–100, 105; Rich). While Sheehan was in Crawford, Texas, holding a vigil for her son and trying to meet with President George W. Bush, the media discovered that Pat Sheehan had filed for divorce and the story was circulated widely that it was because of the vigil (2006b, 180–181). Clearly, this is a painful part of Sheehan's story, so painful that she entitles the chapter in which she explains what happened, "The Death of the Sheehan Family." While this is a chapter that tells the truth behind the divorce, this death is another example of a time when Sheehan will not allow the media or George W. Bush to define the meaning of her life, and she devotes herself again to becoming a mother and to creating a culture of peace.

Transformed Mother

Sheehan's message of love clearly begins with her love for Casey, but her love expands with her activism and transforms who Sheehan is as a mother. Sheehan faces the worst fear imaginable for a mother when her son dies. Even as it devastates her and incapacitates her in being able to care for her other three children in the weeks following his death, she begins to become a new kind of mother, one who is transformed as a result of Casey's death and Carly's poem and one who mothers the "human family."

To understand how Sheehan transforms herself as a mother and challenges stultifying stereotypes of mother, we can begin with Natalie Wilson's article about Sheehan, "From Gestation to Delivery: The Embodied Activist Mothering of Cindy Sheehan and Jennifer Schumaker" (2010). Wilson identifies three key characteristics of Sheehan's activism. First, as

> an 'everymom identity' in order to manipulate this status into what Andrea O'Reilly (2004) (drawing on Adrienne Rich) defines as a 'mother outlaw' identity; second, they invoked a 'personal is political' methodology . . . and third, they enacted what I call 'embodied activism,' a form of activism that resolutely refuses 'abstract rationalism' and instead foregrounds the ways in which national and international policies and institutions affect mothers and their families. (232)

Wilson argues that Sheehan's embodied activism is a strategy employed in many feminist struggles. As part of her review of the history of embodied activism, Wilson points to the extreme physical suffering that Sheehan endures at Camp Casey during the 26-day-long vigil when she endures searing heat, fire ants, thunderstorms, and exhaustion (236). The significance of this embodied activism is that these women use their bodies as a physical manifestation of the harm caused by social injustice.

Sara Ruddick articulates the power of this kind of activism in her article, "Preservative Love." In this article she explains the ways in which mothers have insight into the concreteness of life and living that is in direct contrast to the abstraction that makes militarism and warfare possible. "'Abstraction' refers to a cluster of interrelated dispositions to simplify, dissociate, generalize, and sharply define. Its opposite, which I will call 'concreteness,' respects complexity, connection, particularity, and ambiguity" (2007, 131). Sheehan repeatedly employs this strategy to make visible the hidden costs of warfare by displaying her pain to those who try to keep the costs of war abstract.

When Sheehan explains to readers what she hoped to accomplish in a meeting with Rumsfeld, we can see why this embodied activism conveys a powerful political message. "I wanted [Rumsfeld] to look me in the face and see my red swollen eyes and to see all the lines that grief has etched. I wanted him to see the unbearable pain his ignorance and arrogance have caused my family and me. I wanted him to know

that his actions have terrible consequences" (2005, 11). The political
implications of this imagined interaction carry far more weight than one
mother's loss being conveyed to the person she holds accountable for
her son's death. As Sheehan makes clear throughout her work, she is
the voice of every mother who lost a child in the Iraq War and Rumsfeld is not just responsible for the death of Casey, but for the deaths
of thousands of U.S. soldiers and tens of thousands of Iraqi citizens. In
response to critics who say that she should go home and take care of
her kids, Sheehan responds: "The second reason this command from the
self-righteous right offends me is that I believe that what I am doing
is for my children, and the world's children. I think that the strategy
of eternal, baseless war for corporate profit and greed is bad for all of
our children, born and unborn" (2005, 118). In this passage, Sheehan
rejects the idea that mothering her particular children is separate from
caring for the well-being of all children. Her words also clearly call on
a consistent valuing of all children, whether they are hers or the children of Iraqi mothers, whether they are alive now or will be born in
the future (2006b, 189).

This contrast between caring only for one's own children and
extending that care to all children and all people also applies to the
contrast Wilson draws between maternalist activism and activist mothers. Maternalist activism relies on essentialist understandings of women
and mothering; it reinforces stereotypes about "woman" and "mother"
and can be used to attack activists like Sheehan for not fitting those
stereotypes. Activist mothers, on the other hand, are mothers who rede-
fine mothering in addition to challenging social injustice: "For example,
activist mothers of the early twenty-first century such as Sheehan often
instigated their activism through reference to their role as mothers, but
they did not tend to use this status as the entire grounding for their
aims" (233). If maternalist activism is the standard that one uses to judge
Sheehan's activism, then one would conclude that she fails as a mother.
Wilson describes the ways in which Sheehan subverts stereotypes of
mothering, "[Cindy Sheehan] did not attempt to speak in 'accepted
mother language' that appeals to people's expectations of mothers as
caring, soft-spoken, or domestic. On the contrary, she proved herself to
be argumentative, confident, angry, and rather fond of the f-word" (233).
Moreover, throughout her work Sheehan uses her anger to expose the
truth of the Iraq War and war in general, and she does not hesitate to
use that anger to describe the President and his administration: "This war

was sold to the American people by a slimy leadership with a maniacal zeal and phony sincerity that would have impressed snake-oil salesmen a century ago," and she describes George W. Bush as "the maniac in the White House" (2005, 15, 48).

Instead of chastising Sheehan for not respecting Bush and the office of the president, Wilson calls Sheehan's descriptions of Bush a "matriotic methodology of personalization." Wilson is describing the concretization that Sheehan's experience as a mother allows. Instead of Bush's abstract focus on freedom, democracy, and the War against Terror, Sheehan focuses on the personal disaster that mothers face when their children are killed in pursuit of abstract ideals. Wilson observes: "Further, through her practice of calling President Bush 'George,' Sheehan delivers the message that ordinary mothers (and their soldiering children) deserve as much (or more) respect as government leaders" (241). Wilson's insight into the power of Sheehan's descriptions of Bush, both when she is angry and when she uses his first name, also provides insight into the transformation of mothering that Sheehan enacts. Rather than focusing on a nuclear family isolated from other families, her words and her actions connect her to other mothers and fathers and children; she refuses to stay apathetic and isolated after Casey's death.

Conclusion

Sheehan expands the definition of mothering and peace as she grieves Casey's death and works to end the Iraq War and create a just society. As Wilson writes, "In addition to being criticized for being too political, the perception of Sheehan as a sympathetic grieving mom to crazy, radical leftie undoubtedly also came about due to her transgressing the supposedly normal time limits of grief and the normally privatized role of mother. Mothers, like widows, are supposed to mourn for a certain amount of time, and then they should get on with their lives, which usually means attending to the living children or spouse" (237). Sheehan does pull herself out of her grief and despair, but she does not return to the life that she left as the woman who worked just for her nuclear family. Instead, she begins to work tirelessly for every child. In her reflections on her time at Camp Casey, Sheehan talks about a friend and fellow activist who accompanied her throughout the 26 days, Diane Wilson (2006b, 147–152). Wilson takes the work that Sheehan does and expands the definition of peace even further. Wilson's actions, which I will examine in the following chapter, illustrate that peace is much more than stopping a particular war or even stopping war in general. Peace creates just cultures.

Diane Wilson and the Genealogy of a Bay

In the previous chapters, I have drawn attention to the critique of militarism and injustice and the actions that Molly Rush, Michele Naar-Obed, and Cindy Sheehan performed to bring awareness of injustices and to convince people that one person can make a difference and that we do not have to be complicit with injustice. The culture of militarism that has been the focus of this book is not only about struggling against current wars and potential wars, but it is also about the way in which militarism produces a culture of exploitation that applies to other people and to the world itself. For us to fully think about what a just future and a just society would entail, we can turn to the work of Diane Wilson, who supported Sheehan in her efforts against the Iraq War, prevented further destruction of the bay on which she had spent her life, and linked her local struggles to the struggles of mothers across the world.

The first time I heard about Diane Wilson was through a colleague who recommended Wilson's book, *Unreasonable Woman: A True Story of Shrimpers, Politicos, Polluters, and the Fight for Seadrift, Texas*, and told me she would be speaking on our campus. I had the privilege of reading this book, hearing her speak, and meeting her when I was a mother of three young children. Wilson's story of taking on a huge chemical company that was buying the favor of local people, local and national politicians, and even the Environmental Protection Agency both inspired and terrified me. She inspired me because she is fearless in her pursuit of justice; and she is ultimately successful both on a personal level, because she never wavers from her path even when the practical success seems impossible, and on a practical level, because she gets Formosa and Alcoa, two of these imposing chemical companies, to agree to zero emissions from their plants.

Her story also terrified me because if she can take on these companies and be a force for justice, then what sacrifices should I be willing to endure for the sake of my children and my community? What sacrifices should my children endure for the sake of a just world both for them and for every other child as well? After all, Wilson is the mother of five, two of her children were young enough that she describes them as "babies" when she began her activism, and one of those babies was autistic. Even though I have yet to be, and remain, terrified of the prospect of being as fearless as Wilson—who has been on many hunger fasts, been arrested numerous times, disrupted Senate hearings, and chained herself to a Dow Chemical oxide tower—I tell her story as often as possible as an example of mothering at its best because her story reveals the interconnection between all children and between all people and the environment.

Wilson is a mother and an environmental activist; these two roles challenge common perceptions about what a mother is and what her obligations to her children are, and they also challenge common stereotypes about environmental activists and the focus of their acts. Her story reveals the ways in which mothering is always practiced in a context. Sometimes in order to work toward a society in which her children can thrive, a mother may have to challenge the context itself and take time away from her children. We may be tempted to romanticize motherhood or environmental activism, but the reality of mothering is that in order for our children to live in a world in which they can thrive, the world itself has to be questioned, challenged, and changed, none of which sits well with the few who are in power and for whom the world as it is works well. When Wilson engages in questioning, challenging, and changing the world, she faces pressure from local and state politicians and international business leaders. Her refusal to cooperate with the interests of business at the expense of people and the environment leads her to acts of civil disobedience, which in turn result in jail time and time away from her children.

Militarism and Environmental Destruction

The link between militarism and environmental destruction is an important connection for mothers, feminists, and peace advocates to make. If the connections between different forms of injustice remain hidden, the work of advocates can be dispersed to such an extent that, even when their actions are effective in one area, the structures that support injustice remain untouched. In order to build the kind of future that will be good for all women and for children, the complex interrelationship between various forms of injustice must be exposed such that injustice does not seem to be natural or inevitable. Once the system of injustice is revealed, it becomes possible to choose other forms of living together.

In her article, "Health, Peace and the Environment: Integrating Relationships in Women's Health Movement," Dorothy Goldin Rosenberg traces the history of environmental destruction and militarism in the U.S. military since World War II (25–27). From the use of Agent Orange in Vietnam to the use of depleted uranium in Kosovo, Afghanistan, and Iraq (Carr; Joksimovich), the production and use of weapons are destroying the environment and human health, "These combined 'ecopathologies' [acid rain, ozone depletion, climate change, loss of topsoil, forest destruction, desertification, increased radiation exposure] have resulted in loss of species, increases in the rates of cancer, allergies, asthma and a great number of congenitally damaged children" (Rosenberg 25). Rosenberg's analysis of environmental destruction highlights the connection between militarism, environmental devastation, and undermining the well-being and health of children.

According to Susan Griffin, the very conditioning of the mind of the soldier makes it impossible for soldiers to recognize the environmental destruction or to sympathize with the loss of ecosystems. The poetry she uses to describe the conflict between the training necessary to create a good soldier and the mindset necessary to trace the poisoning of the world calls our attention to the enormity of the task of activists who are working to bring about a just society:

> There are stretches of land scattered throughout the United States that have become so desolate they are the stuff of legends . . . These are the dumping grounds for the United States military, places where the unintended excrescences of wars real and imagined have been hidden, shed, stored . . . Underneath subterranean waters are fouled and carry their poisons unobserved past the gates and sentries into the surrounding countryside, towns, cities / The effects where they have been observed are devastating. / Cancers, childhood leukemias, whole communities uprooted, farms abandoned, unworkable . . . Armies are supposed to defend the people against early, untimely death from unseen enemies . . . How is it then that these visible marks on the land, and the countless less visible traces of danger, escaped notice? . . . The body of a good soldier. Trained to respond quickly to danger. /

And yet at the same time educated away from fear and other
more subtle responses . . . And the quick reactions necessary in battle make the soldier speed past so much texture,
detail . . . Of course, these habits of perception would not
prepare the mind to see the intricate levels of existence in
a field, valley, stretch of desert, forest, at the edge of the
stream. (Griffin 12)

This lengthy passage from Griffin makes the connections between the
emptiness that results from environmental destruction and the way in
which the mind must be trained and disciplined so as to view certain
features at the expense of other features. The human mind will not
necessarily be in tune with sympathy, compassion, and recognition of all
that the natural world makes possible for humans, nor will the human
mind necessarily narrow its focus so that a person is prepared to make
instantaneous distinctions between friend and enemy so that friends
will be protected and enemies destroyed. The mind of the soldier is
cultivated to minimize sympathy for the enemy, and for people not like
"us." While this makes soldiers effective in battle, it makes them inef-
fective in having sympathy for those they do not know who suffer from
the cancers and epidemics caused by poisoned water and soil, let alone
experiencing the sympathies necessary to feel pain for the destruction
of delicate ecosystems.

The preparation for either mindset takes time to develop; both
of these mindsets can be cultivated by mothers. Mothers who cultivate
the mindset necessary to produce a soldier, prepared to fight and kill,
blind to the destruction caused by militarism and weapons, do so out
of love for their children and a misplaced belief that the military can
make people safe. Soldiers' mothers are no less loving and no less concerned for their loved ones' well-being than activist mothers; certainly
Cindy Sheehan demonstrates that it is incorrect to dichotomize these
two groups. In reference to militarism in Canada, which also applies
to the U.S.'s militarism, Murray Thomson makes the observation that
militarism is popular, "because military action in the past was considered to be essential for our survival . . ." and because it requires values
that we hold in high regard. "These values include personal fortitude,
bravery, and a willingness to sacrifice one's life for a higher cause" (38).
For people to overcome the popularity of militarism in favor of creating
a peaceful society will require that they understand that military action
threatens our survival much more than it protects our survival and that

the values that we admire in soldiers are better realized when applied toward fighting injustice nonviolently.

Sara Ruddick describes the motivation of mothers who endorse war and support the military thusly: "Women, a powerless group, may be especially fearful of alleged aggression. In the face of real or imagined threats, weapons can be wonderful, especially if carried by others, while to let one's 'own men' remain unarmed can seem the epitome of vulnerability" (2007, 139). Ruddick's description is important because she does not demonize mothers who raise their children to be soldiers; instead, she recognizes the motivation that they feel to keep their children safe. Because she understands why women would encourage aggression and militarism, she provides a way for mothers working for peace to reach out to other mothers and to find a way to dismantle the largest systems of injustice so that the connections between all children can be safe, instead of pitting some children against others.

Well-known ecological feminist, Victoria Davion, has consistently made connections in her work between environmental destruction and patriarchy; more recently, she has also made the connection between environmental destruction and militarism (Davion 112–125). In "The Earth Charter and Militarism: An Ecological Feminist Analysis," Davion analyzes the United Nations Earth Charter's recognition of the independent value of nonhuman life's implications for military action (117). Davion points out that one of the most significant attributes of the Charter is that, "[i]f the interests of non-human beings are considered, it seems likely that almost no military action could be justified using these principles" (120). Since current military practice relies on the destruction of the environment, as described above, the acknowledgment of the independent value of the environment means that there must be some accounting of the possible destruction of the environment in any military action. The necessity of accounting for costs to the environment creates a pool of knowledge about the true costs of war that are currently hidden when calculations only apply to monetary cost and cost of human life (123–124). The question as to what extent that knowledge is transmitted and used to prevent war is still something that activists will have to confront, since even the value placed on human life is shaped by nationality, ethnicity, race, and class. Wilson's activism on behalf of people in her community and around the world, as well as her activism on behalf of the environment, is precisely the work that provides knowledge, a path to change unjust structures, and a vision of a just society.

Wilson as Mother

In order to think about Diane Wilson as a mother, I will begin by analyzing her descriptions of mothering relationships. As with every mother,
Wilson's story as a mother begins long before she has her own children;
it begins with Wilson as a daughter and a granddaughter. And her story
as a mother is broader than the human relationships she has; it includes
the bay, which she describes as a "grandmother." In this section, I will
explore the influences on Wilson as a mother that lead her to environmental activism.

While it is useful for explanatory purposes to first consider who
Wilson is as a mother and then who Wilson is as an environmental
activist, I want to stress that the two are always intertwined in Wilson's
descriptions of herself. Throughout her memoirs, Unreasonable Woman
and Diary of an Eco-Outlaw, Wilson describes her actions as though her
path is destined. First, she seems to be destined to be a shrimper, and
later she seems destined to be an environmental activist (2005; 2011).
In order to understand the connection between shrimping and environmental activism, it will be important to notice that family for Wilson
includes both people and the environment, and to notice in this section that the genealogical descriptions that appear in Wilson's memoirs
are about her literal genealogy, her blood relatives both maternal and
paternal, and her metaphorical genealogy when she describes Lavaca
Bay as a grandmother.

As a shrimper, Wilson traces her relationship to the bay back to
her grandfather and as a deep part of who she is. Although fishing is
primarily practiced by men—who consider a woman on the bay at best
unusual and at worst courting disaster—Wilson inherits and takes up
the tradition in spite of any pressure for her to stay on the shore. She
describes how inevitable it is that she is an exception to the rule that
only men fish: "everybody knew I was on the bay 'cause my daddy was
on the bay, and my daddy was on the bay 'cause his daddy was on the
bay, and his daddy was on the bay 'cause his daddy had pitched him over
the side of a homemade fishing skiff and said, 'Sink or swim. Swim or
drown. Make up your mind, boy!'" (2005, 49). While she acknowledges
that it is unusual for women to fish, her descriptions remind us that she
feels only a continuity between herself, her family, and the bay.

Her descriptions of fishing and the bay teem with the relationship
between generations, both in the ways in which fishing is passed on
from one generation to the next (2005, 48–54), and also in familial

relationship between the water and those who fish. In his foreword, Kenny Ausbel captures the rich sense of relationship that Wilson has to Lavaca Bay: "Growing up, Diane said the bay was like her grandmother; she spent endless hours in private conversation with her. She took the destruction of the bay very personally. Call it family values" (2011, 11). In her words, Wilson says, "I could see the bay as an old grandmother with long gray hair and a dress made of matted foaming seaweed flowing out with the tide" (2011, 9). The description of the bay as a grandmother is not simply a nostalgic description of the environment, it calls to mind the reality that our life depends on forces beyond us that create the conditions for our lives. Her family's existence relied on the presence of the bay and the health of the bay. For all of us, our physical being is only possible because of our human grandmothers and our mothers. Beyond that, our physical being depends on the environment in which we live. Our particular lives are shaped by the histories and the stories of those who come before us. For Wilson, her love of the bay, of fishing, and of silence are all shaped by her ancestors: some were immigrants, others were Native American (her father's father was Cherokee). All of the people who shape Wilson's identity are, in turn, shaped by the environment.

Of course to think about Wilson as a mother, we have to turn to her descriptions of her children and of herself as a mother. Wilson's children are a constant presence in her life and in her descriptions of becoming an environmental activist. They come with her as she works at the fish house, playing in piles of ice (2005, 53, 114); the older girls come with her to protest against a politician who refuses to take Wilson's calls or acknowledge the petitions that she has sent him against Formosa (2005, 176), they move with her from home to home after she and her husband divorce (2011, 25), and throughout her memoirs Wilson describes her son Crockett's particular ways of moving through the world (2011, 25, 27). She writes about her turn from "reclusive fisherwoman with five kids to controversial hell-raiser with five kids" (2011, 14). I will return to this quote and her turn from recluse to activist in the following section, but for now I want to point out that her identity as a mother with five kids remains constant and shapes every aspect of her story.

Wilson does not detail her children's reaction to her as a woman who refuses to conform to social norms, first by being a shrimper and later by being an activist, but the pull between social norms for mothers and her actions as an activist are evident in several anecdotes that she describes in *Diary of an Eco-Outlaw: An Unreasonable Woman Breaks the*

Law for Mother Earth. Wilson relates several stories in which her family intervenes and tries to get her to give up her activism. In one anecdote, Wilson's mother wants her to stop her activism because she's worried about what will happen to Wilson's children if she dies. Even when her girls are grown and have moved away, and Crockett is sixteen, Wilson's mom tells her: "Kids never grow up" (43), implying that Wilson is a negligent mother for jeopardizing her health through a hunger fast. Later, Wilson describes her aunt's attempt to get her to give up a hunger fast and threatening to bring Crockett to witness the fast. Because Crockett would be upset to see his mother fasting, the aunt hopes that Wilson will stop in order to spare Crockett. Wilson's observation is: "If anyone ever thought that corporations brought in the heaviest gunfire on a hunger strike, they were sadly mistaken. Family and friends beat corporations by a landslide" (55). Of course, neither her aunt nor her mother was successful in getting Wilson to stop her activism, and I will argue that she is the best kind of mother because of this.

The expectation that she will stop her activism if she sees it is harming or could potentially harm her children is based on an understanding of mothering one's particular children as distinct from the harms that happen more generally to the environment or to children who are far away. However, we have already seen that Wilson does not see herself or her children as isolated from the environment. Hence, to be a mother to her children, she will have to defend the environment and other children as well. This connection will be especially clear in the next section when she begins her fight for justice in solidarity with the people of Bhopal, India.

Wilson as Activist

The connection between Wilson, her children, the environment, other people, and places both near and far becomes explicit when she's invited to Bhopal, India, to take part in testimonies against Union Carbide whose mismanagement and business practices had led to explosions in Seadrift, Texas, and Bhopal. The Bhopal disaster killed more than 3,000 people and sickened many thousands (BaoBao). While she is there, her experiences as a mother become part of her response to the suffering of other mothers and the losses that they endure. In *Diary of an Eco-Outlaw*, Wilson describes being on a bus in India as she prepares to give testimony about Union Carbide, Formosa Plastics, and the dangers that these plants pose to people and the environment. While on the bus, a man throws in a handkerchief that contains photos of ten dead babies, laid out on white sheets covered with blood. She discovers that those are photos of babies who were spontaneously aborted by their mothers as they ran from the Union Carbide disaster in Bhopal. These abortions happened as a result of the deadly poisons released in that disaster. She writes that, after seeing these pictures and entering them into evidence against Union Carbide, the connection between those babies and her own children haunted her. "All I knew was that those dead babies with their frail arms flung across the white sheets seemed a whole lot like my own sleeping babies in their cribs at night and when I got back to Texas, those tiny fists pounded me in my dreams and railed against me forgetting" (23). The memory of her own children as vulnerable babies in their cribs reverberates in her response to seeing the babies who were never born, not because they were unwanted but because of the toxic effects of the chemicals from the Union Carbide plant. Rather than forgetting the connection between those babies and her own babies, Wilson directs her considerable energies toward getting other people to remember, as well as calling for the people of Seadrift, Texas, to think about Bhopal and to see connections between Union Carbide's practices in India and Texas, which call attention to the way that human and environmental needs are connected everywhere.[1]

Derrick Jensen, in his foreword to Diary of an Eco-Outlaw, describes Wilson's activities as directed toward delegitimizing corruption and dismantling injustice (ix–xii). By planning disruption, organizing protests, and encouraging others to stop cooperating with injustice, governments and corporations are unable to sustain corrupt practices; however, convincing people to stop cooperating with corporations and governments that are unjust is an incredibly difficult proposition. One of the first things that Wilson's actions reveal in both Unreasonable Woman and Diary of an Eco-Outlaw is that when corporations pollute the environment they spend a great deal of time and money trying to convince people their actions are good for communities because they bring jobs, provide tax revenue, and give charitable contributions (2005, 81). The corporations that Wilson faces, such as Union Carbide, Formosa Plastics, and Dow Chemical, are multinational companies with enormous power and long histories of acting as though laws do not apply to them. For example, when Warren Anderson, CEO of Union Carbide and the person ultimately responsible for the Bhopal disaster, is wanted on a warrant for murder by the Indian government, he is able to flee India and live in the United States because the U.S. government refuses to pursue extradition. Again and again, people ask Wilson what she could possibly hope to accomplish against this kind of power. In the face of these obstacles, most of us cannot imagine risking embarrassment, harassment, and imprisonment in order to challenge business as usual. For Wilson, though, every action disrupts the illusion that these companies are all-powerful, cannot be challenged, and that the outcomes that happen as a result of corporate wrongdoing are inevitable.

Wilson's story of becoming an activist provides a model for how others might also move past being intimidated by these enormous corporations. One of the reasons Wilson is such an inspiration as a mother and environmental activist is that she initially comes to this life reluctantly; she is not born into a life of outspoken activism. All of her descriptions of her early life are descriptions of her love of silence and solitude. She shaped the rhythms of her life with the rhythms of the bay, and when these rhythms were disrupted, she found her love of silence and solitude transformed; she begins to walk an entirely new path.

As someone who has inherited the life of fishing, Wilson is keenly aware of the changes to the environment that shape fishing. Even before Wilson knew about the pollution happening in Calhoun County, she knew that the conditions for fishing and shrimping in Lavaca Bay had changed. She describes a time when shrimpers could find places that hadn't been searched and netted, a time before the bay started to show signs of pollution: red tide, brown tide, green tide, dead dolphins, empty nets (2005, 18–19). As I stressed in the previous section, for Wilson the bay is not only a source of livelihood, it is also a source of life. Even when fishing becomes almost impossible because of the pollution, Wilson describes the need to keep fishing that characterizes the people who fish: "They couldn't quit. But if one did, he never fully recovered. He was a dead man walking" (2005, 19). When Wilson calls a fisherman who quits fishing "a dead man walking," she reminds us of the devastation inflicted on the whole community. The destruction of the bay destroys the way of life that had been passed on through generations and disrupts the conditions for nurturing life from one generation to the next, which is precisely the work of mothering.

Wilson inadvertently discovers the cause of the changes in the bay while working at her brother's fish house, when a fisherman comes in with a newspaper article—which states that Calhoun County has more land toxins than anywhere else in the United States—a statistic that becomes available because industries in the United States had recently been required to report all of their emissions (2005, 36). Initially, Wilson responds in the way that most of us respond to news that seems too awful and too overwhelming for any individual to address: "So I did the only thing you can do after winning something like that. I pretended I never saw the newspaper. It could lie down alongside the rest of the bad news that lined up so well in a dying town" (2005, 27). When Wilson uses the term "winning," she is ironically referring to Calhoun's status as the most polluted county in the United States. As most of us would do upon reading that kind of news, Wilson is tempted to shake her head in disgust and go back to her life as it was before she had read the article.

Unlike most of us, though, Wilson does not stay in a state of denial; she responds to this bad news by taking one step after another to find information, to pass that information on to others, and to act in response to the information that she finds. She describes the day that turned her into an activist in *Diary of an Eco-Outlaw*: "That day is as good as any at explaining why my life turned 360 degrees from reclusive fisherwoman with five kids to controversial hell-raiser with five kids" (14). This description calls us back to the point I want to make about Wilson's work, which is that even though her activism will sometimes take her away from the day-to-day tasks of mothering, it is a life-giving part of her work as a mother. The conditions of her community have undermined her children's possibility of becoming the next generation of fishers and the conditions of the world are undermining the possibility of the next generation to live healthy lives and to find meaningful work.

In order to understand why her actions pose such a challenge to her context and qualify Wilson as a "controversial hell-raiser," I will turn to analysis from Vincent J. Miller in *Consuming Religion: Christian Faith and Practice in Consumer Culture* (2004). As part of his analysis of the difficulties of critiquing and changing social structures that lead to systematic injustice, Miller analyzes the ways in which people's desires are shaped by consumer culture; in particular, he analyzes the way in which the media's portrayals of suffering become a spectacle that conditions us to respond passively to suffering. The media uses suffering in its broadcasts to incite emotion, but the lack of analysis of causes and context of that suffering encourages viewers to accept the visibility of suffering as inevitable and an opportunity to feel shock rather than an opportunity to incite responsive action (130–137). An important part of Miller's analysis is that our response to the suffering that we observe on the news, read about in newspapers, and even see around us is not a selfish, unsympathetic response. Instead, the response to suffering may be quite sympathetic and we are frequently moved to do something about the suffering that we hear about.

Consider, for example, that after Haiti was devastated by an earthquake in January of 2010, people contributed more than $395 million dollars to help the people of Haiti (Ellis). While this sympathy is admirable, donating money does nothing to change the structural problems that made such devastation possible. The news coverage of the earthquake focused on the destruction of that disaster rather than investigating the colonial history that produced gross inequalities in income, lack of infrastructure, and a history of government oppression of Haitians—all of which made the earthquake more devastating than it might have been without Haiti's colonial history. The conclusion Miller draws is that even when our emotional response to suffering leads us to sympathize with others, the structure of consumer culture tends to paralyze our ability to respond because we remain ignorant as to the causes of the suffering. If we cannot understand the history of how that suffering began, then the inequity tends to seem inevitable. If we do not understand the source of suffering, the current disaster seems to be the result of chance rather than of decisions made by people. This inevitability paralyzes our ability to imagine that circumstances could be different, which would lead us to act.

Now, we can consider how different Wilson's actions are as compared to how most people would act upon hearing about the disaster at Bhopal. Most of us, upon seeing pictures of the spontaneously aborted fetuses of women exposed to chemicals, would feel heartsick and wish the explosion had never happened. Wilson, however, links those children and their well-being to the well-being of her own children. She finds ways to draw attention to their plight and the fact that the man responsible for the disaster is being protected by the U.S. government.

When we further apply Miller's analysis to the impact of Wilson's activism, we can see why her work from the outset poses challenges to the status quo. When another shrimper brings her a brief newspaper clipping with information about the levels of pollution in Lavaca Bay, she asks questions, she looks for the context, she looks for the causes. At every step she continues to ask questions and to seek out answers in spite of being told that she won't understand the answers, that she's jeopardizing investment in the area, and that she needs to go back home. Through this investigation she discovers that the difficulties the shrimpers have in finding shrimp is not some mysterious, uncontrollable, and unlucky twist of fate, but that the change in shrimping conditions is

directly related to pollution in the bay. Even when she discovers the link
between fishing conditions and pollution, politicians, business owners,
and lawyers for industry encourage her to consider the pollution as an
unfortunate consequence of "development" and "jobs," suggesting that
fishing is outdated and fishers need to find jobs in the chemical plants.
Rather than assuming that the pollution simply happened to the bay
and cannot be changed, Wilson continues to investigate the causes of
the pollution until she traces it back to its source, Formosa Plastics,
an international corporation that systematically violates environmental
protection laws around the world. She researches their plans to build a
plant in Seadrift, Texas; she researches the relevant laws for permits that
Formosa would need to build its plant; she researches the laws that could
be used to challenge their plans; and she calls meetings to educate the
people who would be affected by the plant. Ultimately, her persistence
leads her to press for zero-emissions from the Formosa plant—a conces-
sion she ultimately gets, even though the company originally claims that
no such technology exists.

Another perspective that helps us to understand Wilson as an
activist is found in Judith Butler's book, *Frames of War: When Is Life
Grievable* (2009). Butler analyzes the frames through which people, especially U.S. citizens, view the world and the relevant questions for our
times. By examining these frames, she reveals the perspectives that allow
people in a society to grieve some deaths and to overlook other deaths,
and her analysis even provides the resources for us to understand the
celebration that accompanies some deaths (Osama Bin Laden's death in
2011, for example). Butler uses this analysis to critique U.S. militarism
and to provide the means to look beyond the frames that we take for
granted in order to live more justly. The analysis she uses to discover and
break free of militaristic frames is applicable in many situations where
the frames we take for granted perpetuate injustice.

I will use Butler's methodology to discover how Wilson's activism reveals unjust frames, and how breaking these frames allows us to
construct just ways to live. The overall point that Butler makes is that
we have to consider the ways in which narratives are framed such that
questions about justice cannot be asked. In order to apply this analysis
to Wilson's activism, we have to consider the ways in which corporations
such as Formosa and Dow Chemical are viewed by the community and
how Wilson's actions disrupt the frame that they try to present.

Again and again, Wilson describes the opposition that she encoun-
ters when she tries to ask questions about the harm the corporations are
doing to the environment. The opposition she faces reveals the way that

these corporations are able to frame their business practices using the language of investment. By highlighting the jobs provided by the plant, these companies are able to portray themselves as good for the community because the people who work there would otherwise be unemployed and without benefits such as health care and retirement. The companies are also able to portray themselves as responsive to the concerns and needs of the community by giving one town a water purifying plant, hosting town picnics, and giving college scholarships. Finally, they are able to control their public image through campaign contributions. The effectiveness of the companies' framing of their image is evident when friends, family, politicians, and business leaders beg Wilson to stop her petitions, her meetings, and her protests because they are afraid that the protests will scare away the anticipated investment in the community.

The willingness of politicians, workers, and of course the owners and managers of these chemical companies to accept this framing makes sense: they have a financial interest in building a plant that produces PVC (Wilson 156–157); further, they can continue their work most easily by remaining ignorant of the effects of that production on the environment, the health of the workers, and the health of the community. One of the most striking and disheartening aspects of Wilson's memoirs is that, in spite of an abundance of evidence of corporate wrongdoing (deliberate dumping of toxic chemicals, hiding the quantity and kinds of chemicals released in the ground and in the air, hiding information about the toxicity of chemicals to which workers are exposed), officials with the EPA, OSHA, and the courts refuse to enforce the laws which have clearly been broken.

Undaunted, Wilson continues to collect evidence and testimony from inspectors, managers, and workers. And, in spite of enormous pressure to be silent, she finds ways to speak out and to get information from governments and corporations who are not accustomed to being questioned, much less defied. The methods that she uses to break the framing depend on the ways in which she builds relationships. First, as I presented earlier, it is her relationship with the bay itself that leads her to investigate the pollution in the bay and the effects of the chemicals going into the bay. Second, her relationship to the other fishermen allows her to break the frame that these chemical plants are good for workers and jobs. The frames of economic development apply to the fishermen as well because they are the ones who have spent their lives on the bay. They notice when the fish that were once plentiful become scarce; they notice when fish and dolphins that should be healthy are floating on the surface and washed up on shores; and they certainly notice when they have to sell their boats and go to work for the chemical companies.

Yet, rather than listening to the testimony that they might offer, politicians blame the problems in the gulf on the fishermen themselves (2005, 160), which means Wilson must also draw attention to the frames which prevent the politicians from taking seriously the harm to the bay and to the fishermen. One way that she draws attention to the frames is by pointing out how much these companies' investments are costing communities. Formosa Plastics, for instance, wants to build a polyvinyl chemical plant in Calhoun County, but in exchange they want millions of dollars in tax subsidies and abatements (2005, 143–148, 157) and no outside interference such as EPA studies of the environmental impact of the proposed plant (2005, 165).

Finally, Wilson dismantles the idea that these chemical companies are good for workers by talking to the workers themselves. Throughout her memoirs, the workers seek out Wilson to provide her with documentation about forged reports, illegally hidden toxins, willful misrepresentation of leaks and spills, and effects of these chemicals on their health. She persistently passes on this information to officials who are reluctant to act; nevertheless, she reveals the systematic choices that companies make to maximize profits at the expense of workers, communities, and the environment.

Fidelity and the Possibility of Success

Throughout this chapter, I have presented Wilson as a woman whose activism is directly related to her work as a mother and experiences of mothering. As a woman whose children have participated in demonstrations with her, witnessed her suffering during hunger fasts, and suffered ill-treatment when they have visited their mother in jail, many people might stand back and declare her a failure as a mother. These same people might also declare her a failure as an activist by looking at the targets of her activism who have escaped prosecution and enforcement for their parts in killing workers, ruining the health of workers and their families, and destroying the environment. Further, one could note that while people such as Tony Hayward, the CEO of BP Oil responsible for the 2010 spill in the Gulf of Mexico, and Warren Anderson, the CEO of Dow Chemical—current owner of Union Carbide—responsible for the

Bhopal tragedy in 1984 and wanted by the Indian government continue to avoid prison, Wilson has been arrested many times and served time in jail over and over again for drawing attention to their illegal actions. In response to those who would say that Wilson fails as a mother and activist, the analysis I have provided demonstrates her success as a mother and activist, and more importantly she demonstrates fidelity to justice.

As I have read the narratives of great activists for peace, from Socrates to Wilson, from Daniel Berrigan to Dorothy Day, from Cesar Chavez to Molly Rush, I am struck by a common theme in the work they do for peace and justice: they work out of fidelity to peace, not out of calculating probability of success. For some of these activists, the inspiration to carry out their actions comes from religious commitment to acting as God would. For others, the inspiration is that the only possibility for creating peace is to be peaceful regardless of the outcome. These activists acknowledge that we can never guarantee that our actions will produce the change we seek, but we can guarantee that doing nothing will perpetuate the current injustice. As Socrates taught almost twenty-five hundred years ago, when we are faced with a choice between a possible good and a certain evil, then the just choice is to opt for possible good.[2]

Rather than choosing a path that she knows will be successful, Wilson stands in solidarity with those who are oppressed. She never knows as she protests, files lawsuits, and goes on hunger strikes if her actions will lead to prosecution of individuals and companies for polluting the environment, ruining the health of workers, and destroying the jobs of those whose livelihood depends on the health of the bay. She knows, though, that if she stays silent, then the companies and politicians will certainly continue what they have been doing. While she has no guarantee that her actions will change these corporations' practices, the only possibility for change is by breaking through the silence and the frames that industries have created and bought for themselves.

Because Wilson acts when she could be silent, listens to those who have been silenced by politicians and corporations, and refuses to let the threat of prison stop her, she is a successful mother. Her example and her life encourage us to make sure our children understand the interconnection between all people and between people and the environment. She shows us that we are capable of much more than we ever knew, when we are part of communities and systems larger than ourselves. Truly acknowledging this interconnection allows us to create conditions in which all children can thrive. She encourages us to take risks and to become better stewards of our world. She rejects a calculus in which the only things worth doing are those things that are guaranteed to pay off; instead she teaches us that what is just is worth doing, regardless of the consequences. She also demonstrates concretely what daily, intimate connection to some part of the natural world, the bay, does to teach interrelatedness itself.

Because Wilson makes CEOs, companies, and politicians accountable for their actions, she is successful as an activist. She is also successful because she is faithful to those whose cause she takes up. She will not settle for what seems to be the best offer simply so that she can say that she has accomplished something, instead she continues to push companies to do more for their workers and the environment. In some instances, her persistence causes companies to change as when the Formosa and Alcoa chemical companies agreed to use zero-emissions at their plants. Additionally, she is successful because she breaks the frames that prevent others from seeing the harms that are being done to them and the harms with which we are complicit when we remain unquestioning and silent.

Mothering

The Power of Critique, Action, and Transformation

When we think about what it means to mother in U.S. society, we have to remember a point that should already be clear from the previous chapters: all mothers have particular experiences, challenges, and strengths that shape how they mother. Mothers are shaped by their race, their class, and their social expectations. As Nancy A. Naples explains in her sociological research on activist-mothering, these mothers develop standpoints within their activism, but also bring their individual perspectives to their communities. Her research on how mothers become activists reveals that reducing their standpoint to either an individual identity or to a shared, community identity misses the interaction between them (340–342).

The political philosopher, Chantal Mouffe, offers such a description of how people's subjectivity develops in relation to the interplay between individuals and the people around them:

> To be capable of thinking politics today, and understanding the nature of these new struggles and the diversity of social relations that the democratic revolution has yet to encompass, it is indispensable to develop a theory of the subject as a decentered, detotalized agent, a subject constructed at the point of intersection of a multiplicity of subject positions between which there exists no a priori or necessary relation and whose articulation is the result of hegemonic practices. (12)

Mouffe argues that subjectivity happens within a context of diverse practices among diverse groups. The practices and groups that make up an individual's subjectivity are not determined by her or him; the practices and groups influence the individual and the individual influences the practices and groups, but no particular individual is the sole determiner of meaning.

Every community is made up of people with differences, and within these communities we organize ourselves and form collective identities. As Mouffe explains, "One of the crucial questions at stake is the creation of a collective identity, a 'we.' In the question 'What shall we do?,' the 'we' is not given but rather constitutes a problem" (50). Creating a collective identity, a "we," happens in a context and as a process. "We" might be a group of people who are opposed to a particular war, such as the Iraq War. In another context, "we" might be a group of people who have come together to bring about their vision of a just society. What both of these groups have in common is that the individual experiences of those within the group have come together for some common purpose.

Cynthia Cockburn engages in similar analysis in *The Space between Us*. In order to understand, *"how peace is done"* (1), Cockburn has engaged in what she describes as "action research" in which she lived with, observed, and interviewed women actively involved in creating peace (3). Through this process, Cockburn came to identify some of the key characteristics of the democratic alliances between women with differences that had previously led to conflict and violence. According to Cockburn, the alliances happened through the intersection of self-identity and collective identity:

> So we expect collective identities, such as gender and national identities, no matter in how essentialist a form they are dressed by politically interested parties, actually to be lived by individuals as *changeable* and unpredictable. And the way they take shape and change is *relational*. In other words, there is not thinkable specification of selfhood that does not have reference to other people, known or imagined. (212)

When we accept that identity is always shaped by relationships, in process, and enacted in different ways by individual people, as Cockburn suggests, then we see that relationships of problematic difference have the potential to become violent or to build toward peace. Cockburn analyzes the alliances between women in conflict zones who build alliances together to overcome violence and to create peace. In this book, I have examined the strategies of women who are forming alliances with imagined partners in other parts of the world. In both cases, women engage in the process that Cockburn describes of overcoming national pressures to think of some women as other and to project their fears and insecurities on to these unknown others (215). The mothers whom I have analyzed in this book engage in civil disobedience and begin the process of transforming national ideas in the United States about the "other" who is threatened by U.S. nuclear weapons, wars, and environmental destruction.

These mothers come together with groups who support their actions that work to create a new society. Sheehan describes her group, which includes Wilson, as *Mi Familia de Corazón*, "my family of the heart" (2006, 91–94). Nevertheless, it is important to remember that these groups include women and men from diverse backgrounds, a feature which is necessary to prevent oppressive relationships. As Cockburn explains: "The arrangements we choose to make for our interactions with each other, the structures and processes we create for our organizations, shape the way we deal with identities. A creative handling of difference is central to democratic process, and democracy disposes towards non-essentializing conceptualizations of identity" (214). The common thread in Cockburn's research with women who formed alliances to overcome deeply entrenched hatreds and violence and Mouffe's political philosophy is the need to resist essentialism, to embrace difference, and to use democratic processes to engage problematic differences.

Mother Activists Balancing Mothering and Activism

The communities that Rush, Naar-Obed, Sheehan, and Wilson create and join are inspiring examples of choosing to be part of a "we," but they do not tell the full story of the groups that make up our lives. In addition to groups that they have chosen, these mothers are also part of the group of mothers in the United States. The social expectations placed on mothers are probably the most unifying experience each of these mothers face. In "Academic Life Balance for Mothers," Michele L. Vancour and William M. Sherman state that there are, "three ways according to which women come to be considered 'good mothers' in U.S. society—by always 'being there' for their children, by engaging in 'family time,' and by 'doing things' with or for their children" (236–237). This article studies pressures faced by academic women in particular, but the authors' descriptions of expectations placed on women as mothers are ideals that are in place for any U.S. mother, not just academic mothers.

While Vancour and Sherman document the ways in which women in academia feel as though they cannot balance their work expectations and mothering expectations, the social pressure is much more intense for

Rush, Naar-Obed, Sheehan, and Wilson. The actions of each of these women required them to give up time with their children in order to make the world a better place for all children, and each woman dealt with social consequences as a result. Rush described her prison time as feeling as though she were dead to her children (Norman 45–46); Sheehan described the assault from conservative popular media and counter-protests demanding that she stop protesting and return home to take care of her surviving children (2005, 118–119); and Wilson described pressure from her mother to take care of her kids instead of risking her life through a hunger strike (2011, 43). Naar-Obed's experience is the notable exception to the narrative of the public pressure that each of the other mothers express. Prior to their turn toward activism, Rush, Sheehan, and Wilson were mothering in the dominant U.S. paradigm in which they were part of a nuclear family and they were the primary caregivers for their children. Naar-Obed's marriage is part of an alternative community and her mothering is part of that community as well, so that even as she serves time in prison she has the support of her immediate family (defined as her community).

The ways in which mothering is used politically can be transformative in society, but the association of mothering and politics can also be subject to stereotypes about mothers. Marsha Marotta, in "Political Labeling of Mothers: An Obstacle to Equality in Politics," uses the term "MotherSpace" to describe the ways in which mothers are labeled to keep them out of politics and instead limited to re-inscribing the status quo: "They [mothers] are soldiers for the dominant discourses of the day that help deploy the narratives that teach mothers the 'rules' of motherhood, illustrating the links among culture, identities and practices" (325). Marotta specifically links the notion of the "good mother" to pressure that all U.S. mothers face, a notion that prescribes selflessness at the expense of political action. Both the terms "soccer mom" and "security mom" are labels used in presidential elections to supposedly characterize how women were voting, but Marotta's analysis of voting patterns reveals that these terms did little to describe women and the complexity of their voting; rather it hid the differences among women as well as their political concerns. The problem with MotherSpace in politics (Marotta cites Mothers Against Drunk Driving as an example) is that "their maternal activism is more about exercising rights to help others than claiming rights for women themselves or furthering the goal of equality for women" (333). What Marotta finds is that the mothers' political action is reduced to reinforcing restrictive stereotypes about women rather than emphasizing political action that will create systematic institutional justice.

Marotta critiques this narrowing of political impact when she writes: "They [mothers] use their relationship with their children to claim a right to call for reform. But at the same time they confine themselves to those efforts; they associate themselves inextricably with children and their identity as mothers; and they exclude less privileged mothers and women who are not mothers" (334). For the women in this book, political action and mothering coincide, but their actions expand notions of mothering beyond narrow stereotypes, and their political actions extend their communities to mothers, other women, and men, as well as across racial, class, and geographic distances. Because they extend their actions beyond stereotypes of mothering and ideals of the "good mother," Rush, Naar-Obed, Sheehan, and Wilson face widespread condemnation for their actions.

We can trace part of the popular condemnation of maternal activism to a misunderstanding of the kinds of choices that mothers have when it comes to mothering. Judith Stadtman Tucker analyzes the popular perception of "choice" in U.S. society in her article, "From 'Choice' to Change: Rewriting the Script of Motherhood as Maternal Activism" (2010). According to Tucker—who viewed popular blogs, websites, and message boards—consumer culture, consumerism, and conservatism have merged together in such a way that the notion that women choose their mothering situations is an ideology used to mask women's isolation in the home and coercive options about mothering. The ideology serves to limit women's options about mothering, rather than opening up discussions about how the actual circumstances of women's lives shape the choices available for women to make. According to Tucker, "In practice, the quasi-feminist rhetoric of maternal choice is entwined with the concept of a free-market system in which the different choices mothers make are an accurate reflection of maternal preferences, rather than an accommodation to the scarcity of viable options" (300). The idea that women can choose not to become mothers if they do not have access to adequate child care, health care, or education unfairly places the burden of an oppressive social system on individual mothers and masks the ways in which race and class limit access to opportunities for some mothers. This rhetoric of choice disguises the ways in which militarism drains resources that would otherwise be available to provide adequate housing, education, and health care. Finally, the rhetoric of choice allows corporations to place profit ahead of sustainability since the focus on individual choice disguises harms to communities and ecosystems.

Tucker's recommendation for uncovering the limits of choice is to construct narratives that reveal its current limits. "To contribute to meaningful social change, our new narrative must eventually reintroduce the framework of fairness by naming cultural and structural barriers to men's full participation in home life and women's full participation in work life, and by underscoring mothers' socio-economic, racial, and cultural diversity and how difference protects or limits women's opportunities for caregiving, economic security, and family formation" (303–304). Her final suggestion for a transformative narrative of change calls for the kind of work that this book performs: "While contemporary maternal discourse is focused almost exclusively on the here and now, an effective change narrative will need to be more future-focused and provide a realistic and attractive picture of what the world will look like for men, women, and children once the motherhood problem is resolved" (304). As I outlined in the introduction, the way to bring about a just and peaceful society requires a critique of current injustice, a vision of what that just and peaceful society would be, and a means to move from here to there. Tucker's hopeful perspective on a picture of the world in which "the motherhood problem is resolved" is attractive for our ideals, but we must also stress that we will always continue to reassess institutions and practices and that we will never have a static, perfect world.

The Need for Perpetual Change

When I say we will never have a static, perfect world, this is a normative statement as much as it is a descriptive statement. The world is a better place if it is continually changing and growing; peace itself requires continual change. Peace is much more than a simple absence of conflict. Peace is the presence of just relations in the world. If peace were simply the absence of conflict, then peace could be maintained by the threat of violence, or, by oppressed groups of people acquiescing in their oppression. Peace requires people to recognize the dignity of other people, the interconnections between people and the world, and the value of diversity in societies. In order to achieve peace, we must engage in what Emmanuel Levinas calls a "perpetual revolution." The perpetual revolution requires that we constantly reevaluate the institutions that are responsible for maintaining justice in our society, guarding against the evil that can lurk in good intentions, and always looking for new ways to include marginalized people and groups.

As an example of the need for perpetual revolution, which guards against evil that taints the good, Roger Burggraeve describes Levinas's example of Stalin's communism, which begins with just intentions and becomes corrupt by elevating an ideal above the worth of individual people. Stalin begins with a legitimate critique: people are suffering under capitalism. He continues with a legitimate means of addressing suffering: a more just society requires that resources be held in common. Though Stalin's intentions may have been good initially, the ideal was held to be more important than individual lives and any particular moment of history, which led to widespread suffering, intolerance, and political tyranny (Burggraeve 86–90). For Levinas, every good idea, principle, and institution carries a similar risk. Even an institution and system that aims to alleviate suffering must be evaluated to ensure that the means reflect the end, such that violence and oppression will always be rejected as a legitimate means to achieving a just and peaceful society.

Burggraeve writes: "Realized justice does not suffice; it is in constant need of correction, revision, and reform. Only in this way can it avoid petrifying its own ethical quality and suffocate in its own opposite. Only thus can it counter the transformation of the good into evil" (2005, 84). From this perspective, justice is a project that begins in the relationships between individual people. Each of the mothers in this book provides examples of the way in which our most personal relationships can inspire us to want to make the world a better place. The love each mother has for her children awakened them to injustice in the world and prepared them to act in ways that would create the conditions for a just world. While these relationships inspired the initial desire for justice, these mothers' actions expanded their care so that they were acting on behalf of every child, including children who have yet to be born.

In an ideal society or even a well-functioning society, the good of some children would not come at the expense of other children. As Sara Ruddick writes: "The more individualistic, hierarchical, and competitive the social system, the more likely that a mother will see the good of her child and her group's children as *opposed* to the good of children of another mother or another 'kind'" (121). The society that Ruddick describes pits mothers against mothers, and the well-being of some children against the well-being of other children is precisely the kind of society that militarism and gross differences in quality of life produce. When Rush, Naar-Obed, Sheehan, and Wilson work for the good of all children, many mothers and popular media portray them as mothers who do not care for their children. These descriptions are only possible because those offering the critiques of these mothers can only imagine the world as it is, a world in which caring for one's own children requires turning one's back on the needs of other children. These mothers imagine a peaceful world in which the connections that link all of us are relationships of cooperation instead of competition such that the success of some is at the expense of others.

An important consideration, though, in how we imagine and build peaceful societies is that we ought to be engaged with a diverse community that includes problematic differences. Cynthia Cockburn, in *The Space between Us*, explains why this is important,

> In trying to create sustainable democratic polities, then, the three women's projects [that Cockburn studied for her book] are involved in helping each other individually to distinguish between dangerous fantasies and reasonable hopes. For the Self to give up its dream with the Other doing so too is impossible or impossible without defeat and debasement. What the women do, in a sense, is respect each other's fears but see these dreams of simple futures for what they are, impediments to a life now. They are also, as collectivities, resisting the seductions of a collapse into false homogeny, taking care not to imagine a total agenda, complete consensus or common language. (229)

Without diversity in collectivities, people can fall prey to imagining a future that is too homogenous, too set on some particular ideal so that people are not ready to engage nonviolently with difference and problems that inevitably arise within societies. To resist violence and to engage in difference peacefully, groups must work together to challenge the individuals within the group and to perpetually assess what is possible now and how they are developing.

The challenge for mothers living in a society that treats connection as competition is that they must struggle and make sacrifices to achieve a peaceful society, and the mothers in this book choose to do so nonviolently and out of the virtue that Ruddick identifies as "peacefulness." She states: "By 'peacefulness' I mean a commitment to avoid battle whenever possible, to fight necessary battles nonviolently, and to take, as the aim of battle, reconciliation between opponents and restoration of connection and community" (122). The ideal of peacefulness is a goal we can apply to all of the actions described in this book. Rush and Naar-Obed target nuclear weapons in order to bring about awareness of nuclear destruction and to wake people up to the reality that a safe world is one without nuclear weapons. While many want to argue that their acts are violent because they destroy property, these women have an understanding of "property" as that which is proper to the flourishing of life. Anything that only exists to destroy life has no claim to the word "property" and is rightly destroyed. Just as medical doctors destroy cancer because its only effect is destructive, these mothers destroy weapons in such a way that no life and no true property is destroyed. Sheehan seeks to create a world in which we recognize that war serves only to create wealth for a few and can never produce peace, democracy, or safety, and that the resources spent on war could instead be spent creating infrastructure that would support peace, democracy, and safety. Wilson extends the critique of militarism to include a critique of environmental destruction; the world she is helping to create will sustain human and nonhuman life for many future generations.

The ideal of peacefulness is one that shapes all of their actions; nevertheless, they also know that peacefulness does not mean that disagreements will simply fade away. As Mouffe states: "One should not hope for the elimination of disagreement but for its containment within forms that respect the existence of liberal democratic institutions" (50). Disagreement provides an opportunity for choice, provides critiques of unjust institutions, and illuminates new paths to pursue justice. Problems develop when disagreement becomes antagonism such that disagreement becomes violent or prevents any action.

The disagreements that happen between groups with divergent views do not necessarily lead to violence and prevent relationships. Chicago Public Radio hosts a radio program, *This American Life*, which explores issues in the lives of U.S. citizens; at times, the program is lighthearted and other times the program takes on serious issues. In one episode, "Nemeses," Ira Glass (the host) interviews Peter Coleman, the Director of the International Center for Cooperation and Conflict Resolution for Teachers College of Columbia University on work he did to help facilitate dialogue between three pro-life activists and three pro-choice activists in Boston after two women were killed in two abortion clinics by a pro-life extremist. In this interview with Coleman and the participants, Coleman notes that the women developed "thick relationships" with each other and the participants talked about the way in which their conversations over six years allowed them to come to respect and like each other. Their relationships helped to restore civility between the two political groups and to take away some of the tinder that was stoking violence between the two groups.

While Coleman stresses the success of the dialogue process, he also points out that the relationships and good will toward one another did not result in the participants coming to the same political conclusions or the same political goals. Rather, the participants' goals became more solidified and polarized. The reason the positions became more polarized is explained by Glass when he summarizes the views of Madeline McComish, one of the dialogue participants: "She said, having to dig deep to explain your reasoning and why you believe what it is that you believe in a group like this, it forces you to crystallize your own views" (2011). In spite of the apparent incredulity in Glass's voice, Coleman emphasizes that the dialogues were a success even though the women's positions became more polarized. Coleman explains why he considers these conversations a success even though they did not produce a common perspective or common agenda:

> Because what did happen is that the rhetoric changed. The conversations that would happen publicly around abortion, around pro-life, pro-choice, lost a lot of the edge and the vitriol in the community that it had prior to the shooting . . . They consciously decided that part of what they had done is contribute to the conditions where an event like this could take place. (Glass)

What is clear from the exchange between Glass and Coleman is that the two have very different interpretations of what is required for success. For Glass, a successful result of the dialogues is to produce a shared perspective or common policy. For Coleman, disagreement about fundamental perspectives on the world is inevitable and desirable. The goal of these dialogues is not to produce a common worldview; the goal is to create the conditions for disagreement and for opposing perspectives that continues to respect the dignity of each person.

While disagreement between groups is desirable in the proper context, another division exists between groups within a liberal, democratic context and groups who refuse to maintain relationships and good will in spite of deep differences. This distinction is the friend/enemy distinction.

Another group becomes an enemy rather than "they" when the group operates outside the rules by which "us" and "them" play and when the group defines itself in opposition to the identity of us and them (Mouffe 2–3). For this book, an enemy is anyone whose actions threaten the flourishing of other groups. Many philosophers argue that the friend/ enemy distinction can be overcome. For some, friend/enemy is overcome by distinguishing between people and their beliefs or actions in order to fight the actions but not the person. This approach is especially helpful in adhering to the imperative to treat all people as ends-in-themselves. Gandhi follows this approach when he cites the Christian imperative to, "[h]ate the sin and not the sinner" (quoted in Fischer 83). From this perspective, action against injustice, violence, and oppression is aimed at both the oppressed and the oppressor. Ideally, the nonviolent action will convert the oppressor and free the oppressed. Mouffe argues that the distinction between friend and enemy should be overcome through political institutions that transform antagonisms into agonistic politics. Agonistic theorists reason that people will always divide themselves into diverse groups with conflicting interests and ideas that will transform into violent conflict unless processes and institutions are in place to resolve the conflicts.

The examples of activism in this book and the forces against which the mothers are struggling indicate that the friend/enemy distinction is as irresolvable as the us-and-them distinction. The challenge is to address the split between friend and enemy with nonviolent actions. While Gandhi's affirmation of separating others' identities from their beliefs helps to maintain the focus on all people's humanity, it is important to also remember that injustice cannot be tolerated and respect for all people's humanity requires noncooperation with injustice. As Ruddick reminds us: "For both pacifism and maternal practice the desirability of a goal is not separable from its being achieved non-violently" (127). While many people treat the imperative to respect everyone's humanity as anathema to justice because many crimes and acts of war are so reprehensible and that they seem to cry out for revenge, mothers and pacifists recognize a deeper truth about the connection between means and ends, which is that the means that we use are the ingredients that will become the end. Even in situations of grave harm, we must act nonviolently, not because it guarantees that nonviolence will change the perpetrator, but because it is the only possibility for change and because violence will guarantee more violence and lead us further away from a peaceful society.

Martin Luther King, Jr.'s description of the biblical imperative to "love your enemy" helps us to articulate how the friend/enemy distinction can be useful for nonviolent practices. King's description begins with a distinction similar to Gandhi's distinction between the person and her or his actions. King writes that one should love "the person who does an evil deed while hating the deed that the person does. I think that this is what Jesus meant when he said 'love your enemies'" (Washington 46–47). His next words, though, make clear that even if King makes a distinction between a person and her or his actions, the group that he is struggling against is not using such a distinction. King writes,

> I'm very happy that he didn't say like your enemies, because it is pretty difficult to like some people. Like is sentimental, and it is pretty difficult to like someone bombing your home; it is pretty difficult to like somebody threatening your children; it is difficult to like congressmen who spend all of their time trying to defeat civil rights. (Quoted in Washington 46–47)

Those who bomb homes, threaten children, and refuse civil rights to others view those against whom they commit violence as enemies. King cannot control the understanding that this other group has of him and other African Americans, but he can control his response and he can refuse to cooperate with these enemies. Out of love for the enemy and for African Americans, he refuses to be complicit with injustice by keeping quiet and allowing the injustice to continue.

The tradition of nonviolence against injustice continues and has been led by mothers in many instances. While it would be demonstrably false to claim that all mothers are nonviolent, it would be useful to return to Ruddick's work on mothering and nonviolence to further consider how the experience of mothering can provide the resources necessary to stand up against oppression without resorting to violence and without resorting to oppressive stereotypes about mothers. In "Preservative Love and Military Destruction: Some Reflections on Mothering and Peace," Ruddick begins with a quote from Dr. Helen Caldicott from 1979 calling on mothers to use their maternal experience and peacefulness for bringing about peace, and while she is sympathetic to the impulse behind the statements, she is also critical of the essentialism of the remarks. Rather than relying on stereotypes of women as maternal and peaceful, Ruddick points out that women may support war, both by fighting directly or preparing their sons to fight. Further, she reminds the reader that praising women's peacefulness can be a weapon of patriarchy to keep women from having public effectiveness and speaking out against oppression that they and their children suffer. Nevertheless, Ruddick argues that mothers do have a tradition of peacemaking that can be called upon and strengthened and that it is necessarily political (114–116).

In this article, Ruddick points to concrete thinking as perhaps the most definitive attribute of maternal thinking that can contribute to a peaceful society. In answering the question why is maternal thinking necessarily concrete, Ruddick writes: "In short, her thinking will be 'holistic,' 'field-dependent,' 'open-ended,' not because of any innate sex differences, but because that is the kind of thinking her work calls for" (131). The daily work of mothering will always bring mothers back to concrete demands since every day children need to be fed, to be clothed, and to be bathed. Many other days call for other physical demands when children need extra care: changing bedding, cleaning vomit, bandaging cuts and scrapes, or holding and comforting children as they recover from injury or sickness. Mothers have to adapt their care to account for the differences of each child whether it is the differences in personality of children, or the differences in physical ability. Even when mothers apply abstract ideals to their mothering or abstract hopes for their children, these ideals are always part of concrete reality.

The emphasis on concrete thinking that mothers develop is in direct contrast to the abstraction necessary in militarism according to Ruddick. She theorizes that, "We may be able to fight only if war remains an abstract idea; we may forgive ourselves for fighting only because we can resort to the idea of a 'just war' to legitimize our violence" (132). If Ruddick is correct that abstracting the idea of war from the actual effects of war allows war to take place, then this abstraction ought to be apparent in each of the studies in this book, and the mothers' actions ought to disrupt that abstraction. Certainly, the buildup of nuclear weapons during the Cold War revealed a deeply embedded abstraction since an actual war and the threat of Communism is only theoretical. The abstraction is also helped by the idea that nuclear weapons are a "deterrent" because those who build the weapons do not have to think about the effects of these weapons on others since the belief is that manufacturing the weapons will deter war and keep the weapons from ever being actually used. For Sheehan, war and its harms are only too real. Nevertheless, evidence of abstraction is evident in that in spite of a lack of concrete evidence of weapons of mass destruction or a link between al-Qaeda and Saddam Hussein that George W. Bush was able to convince the popular media, congress, and much of the United States (although, tellingly, he did not convince the UN or a multilateral military contingent) that Hussein had a part in 9/11 and that he had weapons of mass destruction that he would use. Wilson helped Sheehan reveal the abstractions of the Iraq War as well as those being used to destroy the environment since companies promised jobs and that they would protect the environment in spite of long, ugly histories of destroying the health of workers and the ecosystems where their plants are located.

The concrete effects that each of these mothers accomplished through their activism can be described using a statement from Cindy Sheehan. "We finally remembered something that we had forgotten after so many years of tyranny and oppression: We the people of the United States of America have the power. Our governments govern only with the permission of the people" (2006, 155). The everyday abstractions of freedom, democracy, patriotism, and security all tend to come together and leave people feeling powerless over our lives; we leave decisions about war and the environment to politicians and corporations and forget that one person can make a difference, one person can be a catalyst for a movement that empowers us and changes the possibilities for the future by changing the choices that we make every day.

Notes

Chapter 5

1. The hunger strike that I referenced in the previous section was done in support of the victims of the Bhopal disaster and their quest for justice.

2. *The Apology.* In this text, Socrates argues that keeping silent to avoid death would be a false form of knowledge. We cannot know whether death is good or evil, but we know that keeping silent about injustice is evil. Since death might be good or might be evil, it is better to avoid what we know is evil rather than act as though we know death will be evil. He goes on to argue in the text that death is probably good, which further indicates that death is not the worst thing that can happen to a human; for instance, letting injustice happen is worse.

Works Cited

"FLA Highlights Underlying Challenges of Child Labor After Extensive Investigation of Nestle Cocoa Supply Chain." June 29, 2012. <http://www.fairlabor.org/blog/entry/fla-highlights-underlying-challenges-child-labor-after-extensive-investigation-nestl%C3%A9>.

"History of the War." *Invisible Children*. 2012. <http://invisiblechildren.com/about/history/>.

"Lords of Woe." *Economist* 397.8708 (2010): 57–58.

"National Priorities Project: Military Recruiting 2006." *National Priorities Project*. December 22, 2006. <http://www.nationalpriorities.org/Publications/Military-Recruiting-2006-2.html>.

"Prisoners of Conscience." *Progressive* 58.1 (1994): 15.

"Tracing the Bitter Truth of Chocolate and Child Labor." March 24, 2010. <http://news.bbc.co.uk/panorama/hi/front_page/newsid_8583000/8583499.stm>.

"US Arms Plan." *U.S.News & World Report* 98.6 (1985): 33.

Aday, Sean, Steven Livingston, and Macye Hebert. "Embedding the Truth: A Cross-Cultural Analysis of Objectivity and Television Coverage of the Iraq War." *Harvard International Journal of Press/Politics* 10.1 (2005): 3–21.

Aldridge, Janet, et al. "Testimonies." *American Spirtualities: A Reader.* Ed. Catherine L. Albanese. Bloomington: Indiana University Press, 2001. 363–81.

Alonso, Harriet Hyman. *Peace as a Women's Issue: A History of the U.S. Movement for World Peace and Women's Rights.* 1st ed. Syracuse, NY: Syracuse University Press, 1993.

Bangura, Abdul Karim. "The Politics of the Struggle to Resolve the Conflict in Uganda: Westerners Pushing their Legal Approach Versus Ugandans Insisting on their Mato Oput." *Journal of Pan African Studies* 2.5 (2008): 142–78.

BaoBao, Zhang. "Five Things You Need to Know about the Bhopal Disaster." *PBS.org.* June 8, (2010). <http://www.pbs.org/wnet/need-to-know/five-things/the-bhopal-disaster/1316/>.

Baraitser, Lisa. "Oi Mother, Keep Ye' Hair on! Impossible Transformations of Maternal Subjectivity." *Studies in Gender & Sexuality* 7.3 (2006): 217–38.

Beauvoir, Simone de. *The Ethics of Ambiguity.* Trans. Bernard Frechtman. Vol. C-107. Secaucus, NJ: Citadel Press, 1948.

Bjorken, Johanna. *Climate of Fear: Sexual Violence and Abduction of Women and Girls in Baghdad.* Vol. 15. New York: Human Rights Watch, 2003.

Boykoff, Jules. *Beyond Bullets: The Suppression of Dissent in the United States.* Oakland, CA; Edinburgh: AK Press, 2007.

Brown, Anna, and Mary Anne Muller. "The Plowshares Eight: Thirty Years On." September 9, 2010. <http://wagingnonviolence.org/2010/09/the-plowshares-8-thirty-years-on/>.

Buirski, Jeannette. "How I Learnt to Start Worrying and Hate the Bomb: The Effects of Nuclear Bombardment." *Over our Dead Bodies: Women Against the Bomb.* Ed. Dorothy Thompson. London: Virago Press, 1983. 15–28.

Burggraeve, Roger. "The Good and its Shadow: The View of Levinas on Human Rights as the Surpassing of Political Rationality." *Human Rights Review* 6.2 (2005): 80–101.

Bush, George W. *Proclamation 8140—Mother's Day,* 2007.

Butler, Judith. *Frames of War: When is Life Grievable?* New York, London: Verso, 2009.

Carr, Paul. "'Shock and Awe' and the Environment." *Peace Review* 19.3 (2007): 335–42.

Catholic Church. Pope (1978– : John Paul II), and John Paul. *The Gospel of Life: Evangelium Vitae: Encyclical Letter.* Boston: Pauline Books and Media, 1995.

Cavell, Stanley. *A Pitch of Philosophy: Autobiographical Exercises.* Cambridge, MA: Harvard University Press, 1994.

Chernoff, F. "Ending the Cold War: The Soviet Retreat and the US Military Buildup." *International Affairs* 67.1 (1991): 111.

Chin, Chuanfei. "Margins and Monsters: How some Micro Cases Lead to Macro Claims." *History & Theory* 50.3 (2011): 341–57.

Cockburn, Cynthia. *The Space between Us: Negotiating Gender and National Identities in Conflict.* London; New York: Zed Books, distributed in the USA exclusively by St. Martin's Press, 1998.

Dakss, Brian. "Army Recruiters Face Investigation." February 11, 2009. <www.cbsnews.com>.

Davion, Victoria. "The Earth Charter and Militarism: An Ecological Feminist Analysis." *Worldviews: Environment Culture Religion* 8.1 (2004): 112–25.

Davis, Angela Y. *Abolition Democracy: Beyond Empire, Prisons, and Torture.* 1st ed. New York: Seven Stories Press, 2005.

Di Leonardo, Micaela. "Morals, Mothers, and Militarism: Antimilitarism and Feminist Theory." *Feminist Studies* 11.3 (1985): 599–616.

Doom, Ruddy, and Koen Vlassenroot. "Kony's Message: A New Koine? the Lord's Resistance Army in Northern Uganda." *African Affairs* 98.390 (1999): 1.

Ellis, Blake. "Haiti Donations Exceed $395 Million." *CNN.* January 21, 2010. <http://money.cnn.com/2010/01/21/news/international/haiti_donations/>.

Engstrom, Nicholas. "The Soundtrack for War." *Columbia Journalism Review* 42.1 (2003): 45.

Enloe, Cynthia H. *Does Khaki Become You?: The Militarisation of Women's Lives.* 1st ed. Boston, MA: South End Press, 1983.

Farhi, Paul. "Everybody Wins." *American Journalism Review* 25.3 (2003): 32.

Faulk, Erin. "PatchPeople: Activist Molly Rush Wins Governor's Award." *Dormont-Brookline Patch.* November 28, 2011. <http://dormont-brookline.patch.com/articles/patchpeople-activist-molly-rush-wins-governor-s-award>.

Fischer, Louis, ed. *The Essential Gandhi: An Anthology of His Writings on His Life, Work and Ideas.* 2nd ed. New York: Vintage Books, 2002.

Fischer, John Martin. *Our Stories: Essays on Life, Death, and Free Will.* Oxford; New York: Oxford University Press, 2009.

Fraser, Barbara. "Peru: Environmental Health as an Equity Issue." *Extractives and Equity: An Introductory Overview and Case Studies from Peru, Angola, and Nigeria.* Ed. Tom Bamat, Aaron Chassy, and Rees Warne. Baltimore, MD: Catholic Relief Services, 2011.

Glass, Ira. *Nemeses.* Chicago Public Radio, 2011.

Griffin, Susan. "Inheritance of Absence." *New Internationalist* 261 (1994): 12.

Gross, Judy. "Peace Activist is in Prison for Child's Sake." *National Catholic Reporter* 33.41 (1997): 5.

Hagopian, Amy, and Kathy Barker. "Should we End Military Recruiting in High Schools as a Matter of Child Protection and Public Health?" *American Journal of Public Health* 101.1 (2011): 19–23.

Hawksley, Humphrey. "Nestle 'Failing' on Child Labour Abuse, Says FLA Report." *BBC.* June 29, 22012. <http://www.bbc.co.uk/news/world-africa-18644870>.

Hefling, Kimberly. "AP IMPACT: Small Towns Bear the Emotional Scars from Iraq." *The Associated Press State & Local Wire.* February 20, 2007.

Irigaray, Luce. *Je, Tu, Nous: Toward a Culture of Difference.* New York: Routledge, 1993.

———. *I Love to You: Sketch for a Felicity within History.* New York: Routledge, 1996.

———. *Democracy Begins between Two.* New York: Routledge, 2001a.

———. *To be Two.* New York: Routledge, 2001b.

———. *Between East and West: From Singularity to Community.* New York: Columbia University Press, 2002.

———. *Key Writings.* Ed. Luce Irigaray. New York: Continuum, 2004a.

———. *Luce Irigaray: Key Writings.* London; New York: Continuum, 2004b.

———. *Sharing the World.* London; New York: Continuum, 2008.

Ismael, Shereen T. "The Lost Generation of Iraq: Children Caught in the Crossfire." *International Journal of Contemporary Iraqi Studies* 2.2 (2008): 151–63.

Jacobs, Amber. "The Potential of Theory: Melanie Klein, Luce Irigaray, and the Mother-Daughter Relationship." *Hypatia* 22.3 (2007): 175–93.

Joksimovich, Vojin. "Militarism and Ecology: NATO Ecocide in Serbia."
      Mediterranean Quarterly 11.4 (2000): 140.

King, Martin Luther, Jr. "Letter from Birmingham Jail." *A Testament of Hope:
      The Essential Writings and Speeches of Martin Luther King*. Ed. James M.
      Washington. San Francisco: Harper San Francisco, 1986. 289–302.

Kitzinger, Sheila. "Sheila Kitzinger's Letter from Europe: Birth, Military
      Occupation, and Patriarchy." *Birth: Issues in Perinatal Care* 32.3 (2005).

Knudson, Laura. "Cindy Sheehan and the Rhetoric of Motherhood: A Textual
      Analysis." *Peace & Change* 34.2 (2009): 164–83.

Lane, Richard. "Northern Uganda: Looking for Peace." *Lancet* 370.6904 (2007):
      1991–2.

Lehrer, Keith. "Stories, Exemplars, and Freedom." *Social Theory & Practice* 37.1
      (2011): 1–17.

Lloyd, Genevieve. "The Self as Fiction: Philosophy and Autobiography."
      Philosophy and Literature 10.2 (1986): 168–85.

Managhan, Tina. "Grieving Dead Soldiers, Disavowing Loss: Cindy Sheehan
      and the Im/Possibility of the American Antiwar Movement." *Geopolitics*
      16.2 (2011): 438–66.

Mariscal, Jorge. "The Poverty Draft." *Sojourners* 36.6 (2007): 32–35.

Miller, Vincent Jude. *Consuming Religion: Christian Faith and Practice in a
      Consumer Culture*. New York: Continuum, 2004.

Mollin, Marian. "Peace Mom: A Mother's Journey through Heartache to
      Activism—by Cindy Sheehan." *Peace & Change* 34.3 (2009): 345–9.

Moravec, Michelle. "Another Mother for Peace: Reconsidering Maternalist
      Peace Rhetoric from an Historical Perspective, 1967–2007." *Journal of
      the Motherhood Initiative: Mothering, Violence, Militarism, War and Social
      Justice* 1.1 (2010): 9–29.

Mouffe, Chantal. *The Return of the Political*. London; New York: Verso, 1993.

Naar-Obed, Michele. *Maternal Convictions: A Mother Beats a Missile into a
      Plowshare*. Maple, WI: Laurentian Shield Resources for Nonviolence, 1998.

———. "Nonviolent Peace Activism." *Social Justice* 30.2 (2003): 119–22.

Naples, Nancy A. "Women's Community Activism: Exploring the Dynamics
      of Politicization and Diversity." *Community Activism and Feminist Politics:
      Organizing Across Race, Class, and Gender*. Ed. Nancy A. Naples. New
      York: Routledge, 1998a. 327–49.

———. *Grassroots Warriors: Activist Mothering, Community Work, and the War
      on Poverty*. New York: Routledge, 1998b.

National Priorities Project. "Cost of War: Trade-Offs." *National Priorities Project*.
      2014. <http://costofwar.com/tradeoffs/>.

Norman, Liane Ellison. *Hammer of Justice: Molly Rush and the Plowshares Eight*.
      Pittsburgh, PA: Pittsburgh Peace Institute, 1989.

O'Neill, Patrick. "Cindy, Other Mothers Speak their Message." *National Catholic
      Reporter* 41.42 (2005): 6.

Okasha, A. "Mental Health and Violence: WPA Cairo Declaration—International Perspectives for Intervention." *International Review of Psychiatry* 19.3 (2007): 193–200.

Rich, Frank. "The Swift Boating of Cindy Sheehan." *New York Times* August 21, 2005.

Rosenberg, Dorothy Goldin. "Health, Peace and the Environment: Integrating Relationships in Women's Health Movement." *Women & Environments International Magazine*. 60 (2003): 25–7.

Roy, Arundhati. *An Ordinary Person's Guide to Empire*. Cambridge, MA: South End Press, 2004.

Ruddick, Sara. "Making Connections between Parenting and Peace." *Mother Matters: Motherhood as Discourse and Practice*. Ed. Andrea O'Reilly. Toronto, Ontario: Association for Research on Mothering, 2004.

———. "Preservative Love and Military Destruction: Some Reflections on Mothering and Peace." *Maternal Theory: Essential Readings*. Ed. Andrea O'Reilly. Toronto: Demeter Press, 2007. 114–44.

Ruddick, Sara. *Maternal Thinking: Toward a Politics of Peace; with a New Preface*. Boston: Beacon Press, 1995.

Sachs, Lynne, dir. *The Catonsville Nine: Investigation of a Flame*. 1 videocassette (45 min.). First Run/Icarus Films, 2003.

Sartre, Jean Paul. *Being and Nothingness: An Essay on Phenomenological Ontology*. New York: Washington Square Press, 1966.

Segal, David R., and Mady Wechsler Segal. *America's Military Population*. Vol. 59. Population Reference Bureau, 2005.

Sheehan, Cindy. *Not One More Mother's Child*. Kihei, HI: Koa Books, 2005.

———. *Dear President Bush*. San Francisco, CA: City Lights, 2006a.

———. *Peace Mom: A Mother's Journey through Heartache to Activism*. New York: Atria Books, 2006b.

The Food Empowerment Project. "Slavery in the Chocolate Industry." 2010. <http://www.foodispower.org/slavery_chocolate.htm>.

Thompson, Dorothy. *Over our Dead Bodies: Women Against the Bomb*. London: Virago, 1983.

Thomson, Murray. "With Militarism being so Destructive, Why is it so Popular?" *CCPA Monitor* 15.3 (2008): 38–41.

Tomchick, Maria. "Powell's Flimsy Evidence." *Z-Net* (Feb. 9, 2003).

Tucker, Judith Stadtman. "From 'Choice' to Change: Rewriting the Script of Motherhood as Maternal Activism." *21st Century Motherhood: Experience, Identity, Policy, Agency*. Ed. Andrea O'Reilly. New York: Columbia University Press, 2010. 293–309.

Tyler, Ann S. "Youths in Rural U.S. are Drawn to Military." *The Washington Post*, Friday, November 4, 2004, sec. A:01.

UN General Assembly. *Convention on the Rights of the Child*. Vol. 1577. UN General Assembly, 1989.

———. "Convention on the Rights of the Child: Frequently Asked Questions." UN General Assembly. February 10, 2006. <http://www.unicef.org/crc/index_30229.html>.

Vancour, Michele L., and William M. Sherman. "Academic Life Balance for Mothers: Pipeline of Pipe Dream?" *21st Century Motherhood: Experience, Identity, Policy, Agency*. Ed. Andrea O'Reilly. New York: Columbia University Press, 2010. 234–46.

Vindevogel, Sofie, et al. "Forced Conscription of Children during Armed Conflict: Experiences of Former Child Soldiers in Northern Uganda." *Child Abuse & Neglect* 35.7 (2011): 551–62.

Wachowski, Andy, dir. *The Matrix*. Warner Home Video, 1999.

Washington, James M., ed. *A Testament of Hope: The Essential Writings of Martin Luther King, Jr.* San Francisco: Harper & Row, 1986.

White, Josh. "Violations by Military Reuiters Up Sharply." August 15, 2006. <www.washingtonpost.com>.

Wilson, Diane. "Diary of an Eco-Outlaw: An Unreasonable Woman Breaks the Law for Mother Earth." (2011).

———. *An Unreasonable Woman: A True Story of Shrimpers, Politicos, Polluters, and the Fight for Seadrift, Texas*. White River Junction, VT: Chelsea Green Pub., 2005.

Wilson, Natalie. "From Gestation to Delivery: The Embodied Activist Mothering of Cindy Sheehan and Jennifer Schumaker." *Mothers Who Deliver: Feminist Interventions in Public and Interpersonal Discourse*. Ed. Jocelyn Fenton Stitt and Pegeen Reichert Powell. Albany, NY: SUNY Press, 2010. 231–52.

Woehrle, Lynne M., Patrick G. Coy, and Gregory M. Maney. *Contesting Patriotism: Culture, Power, and Strategy in the Peace Movement*. 1 pbk ed. Lanham, MD: Rowman & Littlefield, 2009.

York, Byron. "Cindy's Movement." *National Review* 57.16 (2005): 20–2.

Zunes, Stephen. *Afghanistan Five Years Later*. Vol. 43, 2006.

Žižek, Slvoj. "Welcome to the Desert of the Real!" *South Atlantic Quarterly* 101.2 (2002): 385.

Index